UNWOR†HY

JAYMEE WALLACE

THIS BOOK IS PUBLISHED BY LOST POET PRESS

All rights reserved, including the right to reproduce this book or portions of this book in any form whatsoever.

Text copyright © 2025 by Jaymee Wallace

Cover art by Rob Stainback and Jaymee Wallace

For information about special bulk purchases, please contact www.thehealinghubministry.com

Scripture quotations marked (NLT) are taken from the Holy Bible, New Living Translation,
Copyright ©1996, 2004, 2015 by Tyndale House Foundation.
Used by permission of Tyndale House Publishers, Inc., Carol Stream, Illinois 60188. All rights reserved.

Scripture quotations marked (NIV) are taken from The Holy Bible, New International Version®, NIV®.
Copyright © 1973, 1978, 1984, 2011 by Biblica, Inc.
Used with permission of Zondervan. All rights reserved worldwide. www.zondervan.com

Scripture quotations marked (NKJV) are taken from the New King James Version®.
Copyright © 1982 by Thomas Nelson.
Used by permission. All rights reserved.

Published in the United States by Lost Poet Press
First paperback edition.

No part of this publication may be reproduced, stored in a retrieval system, or transmitted in any form or by any means, electronic, mechanical, photocopying, recording, or otherwise, without written permission from the publisher.

www.thehealinghubministry.com

ISBN: 978-1-944470-24-1

This book is dedicated to my mother, Yvonne Marie Lane.

Eight years of praying for Craig and I and one invitation to church on Mother's Day 2005 changed the trajectory of our lives. A new legacy was written because of the power of a praying mama.

Mom, I love you so very much.

FOREWORD

When I first read Jaymee's story, something altogether unexpected happened. An unmistakably divine weight seemed to settle over the moment, over the words she had written, over the very place where I sat. Tears that were mine and yet somehow everyone else's also burned heavy in my eyes. Time slowed in some mysterious obedience to this enchanted moment, and I was speechless.

I could not bring myself to taint the occasion with words, could not spoil the experience with a reaction. I could only sit, in stillness and silence, and bear witness to the incomprehensible grace of God that had led Jaymee to a freedom most of us could only dream of experiencing.

What had I just read?

I would sit there for hours, wrestling with the startling implications of Jaymee's courage and God's goodness. If His mighty hand could work so powerfully through her darkest sins brought into blazing light, how could I possibly justify concealing my own? I watched in awful surprise as Jaymee's courage forged a space as inviting as it was convicting, challenging me to reexamine my own polished and sanitized testimony.

Here was my sister, who with her most shameful moments made mercilessly public, chose not to run away from this but rather to lean in and let God redeem it for her good and His glory.

Here was my sister, who dared to really *believe* that Jesus had fully forgiven her, and lived that belief out in her free sharing of her unfiltered story.

Here was my sister, who had come to rest in Christ's identity despite knowing how her scars and scarlet letters distorted the way other people see her.

Here was my sister, both weary and refreshed from traveling a narrow road that most of us won't set foot on because we fear what it will cost.

Here was my sister.

When the divine experience finally gave way and the comingled tears retreated, I knew what had to happen next: her story needed to be told.

And by God's grace, here it is. In all its flawed and scandalous and improbable glory. As you read it, my prayer is that you too will be stunned into silent wonder at the magnificent grace of God, and that you too will find that her courage forges a space in your own life, inviting you to be vulnerable and brave.

May you discover what Jaymee has long known with life-changing conviction – that when the Son sets us free, *we are free indeed*.

Kara A. Kennedy
August 31, 2025
Lutz, Florida

CONTENTS

FOREWORD iii

INTRODUCTION 1

CHAPTER ONE: DADDY ISSUES 6

CHAPTER TWO: PERFECT PERFORMANCE 17

CHAPTER THREE:: SHAMEFUL SECRETS......................... 28

CHAPTER FOUR: I'M FINE, EVERYTHING IS FINE 39

CHAPTER FIVE: SPIRALING INTO THE MUD 49

CHAPTER SIX: THE TRUTH WILL SET YOU FREE.......... 60

CHAPTER SEVEN: FROM WILDERNESS TO WONDER 67

CHAPTER EIGHT: PRISON PRESSURE 82

CHAPTER NINE: CHURCH HURT AND THE FEAR OF MAN........100

CHAPTER TEN: RESCUED BY GRACE................................ 116

EPILOGUE: FINISHING THE RACE WITH RESILIENCE 126

ACKNOWLEDGEMENTS TO A COMMUNITY OF GRACE............138

INTRODUCTION

"I am not good enough."

Five little words. They pack quite the punch, don't they? These five little words became a mantra for me in the early years of my life. I believed them to the core of who I was. And they nearly destroyed me.

These five little words created a belief system of unworthiness, formed by my experiences of childhood abuse and affirmed by years of relational dysfunction. I grew up tormented by my fear of failure, and this driving theme of deficiency led me to become a self-fulfilling prophecy. Sexual sin, infidelity, and secret shame were not even the worst of it; my unraveling took me through seasons of public humiliation, separation from my precious family, and a lifetime of judgement by others. Were it not for the grace of God, this mantra of shame and unworthiness could certainly have taken my life.

And yet, I've discovered that I'm not the only one. These five little words are a common lie, a falsehood that has devastated the lives of countless individuals. This lie keeps us from God, causes us to suffer in silence, dims our internal light, and keeps us stuck in our shame, unworthiness, and loss of purpose. It is a lie crafted by the enemy of our souls. It is a perfectionist's mantra, one that pushes us to motivate ourselves to be "more" and "better" to prove we are worthy. This lie leads us to seek approval and fear failure: after all, if I fail, that means I *am* a failure. It's identity suicide.

Those five little words are the playlist that never shuts off. Repeated in our minds, over and over again, the torment worsens. We have plenty of evidence to support the theory: our failures, sins, fears, or bad things that have happened to us. As if that weren't enough, we have the people in our lives who have spoken these words over us, to us, and about us. We hunger in the depths of our souls to be loved and known and accepted, yet we can't seem to measure up. And then one day, because we have heard it so frequently, something within us gives up. We come into agreement with the lie, and we believe it. This is now our truth.

"I am not good enough."

This counterfeit, so-called truth is a warped filter on the way we perceive God, ourselves, and our lives. A filter of lies. **A false identity**. This faulty belief system leads us to fill our emptiness with false gods, numb our pain with sin, bow down to the opinions of others, and find our worth in our performance. All of this serves to only pull us further and further away from the only one who can make us whole. We run from God and often blame Him for the outcome of our own faulty belief system.

But it doesn't have to be this way.

Lean in, dearest reader. I have written this book for you, or maybe for someone you love who needs a message of hope. I have lived a story of devastation and destruction. I have lived a story of pain and suffering, sin and shame, failure and loss. I have lived the lie. But that is not where my story ends. I have also lived a story of hope and healing, of grace and goodness. I have lived a story of redemption, a story that takes my shame and transforms it into a testimony of God's mercy and restoration.

I want to tell you my story, because I believe that it may serve to unlock a truth that is rooted deeper than the lies of unworthiness: the truth that you are beloved. My goal in sharing my story is to expose the lies of the enemy and to help you realign any faulty belief systems you have been standing on. I invite you to open your heart with courage, and to consider the possibility that the God who created you *loves you* with an everlasting love, a love that is not contingent on anything you do. I pray that my story might welcome you into a space of freedom and abundant living.

> *"The thief does not come except to steal, and to kill, and to destroy. I (Jesus) have come that they may have life, and that they may have it more abundantly."*
>
> **John 10:10 NKJV**

At center stage of this book, I will be sharing my own real, raw, authentic testimonies with the hope that you will feel safe to come out of hiding. No more masks. No more pretending to have it all together. No more bowing down to pride, fear, shame, and all the lies. You cannot heal what you conceal. The broken version of you will have more use by God than the polished, social media version of you ever could. Your healing isn't just about you. God wants you to help lead others to the same joy, peace, freedom, and abundant life. Someone else's healing is waiting on your choice to courageously take Jesus' hand and deal with your "stuff." It's ugly, it's messy, it's painful at times, but you will be so grateful that you did. God's promises are true for every child of God, and you, dearest reader, are indeed a child of God. You bear the image of your Creator, and only He can define your value.

Spoiler alert: He already has, and your value is infinite.

I pray that as you read this, God will begin to do a deep healing of the broken places of your soul so you can walk in your full inheritance as a child of God.

This book is an invitation. It's an invitation to experience the love of a living, all-powerful God who wants to heal every broken place in your heart. Should you choose to accept His invitation, you will discover His forgiveness, grace, mercy, freedom, and restoration. This encounter will be both comforting and challenging at the same time. His truth will shatter the lies of shame, pride, unworthiness, unbelief, and fear. His love will bring light into the hurting and broken places of your soul. This divine encounter will invoke the power of God and His transforming grace in the life of anyone willing to receive.

There are three ways to engage this invitational memoir. Some will simply read the book from front to back and, through the story, God will stir your heart and increase your faith to bring needed healing. Others may choose to read this book with a small group, engaging in some discussion questions that align with each chapter. These questions can be accessed via www.thehealinghubministry.com. This is to help further fellowship and share in community what God is speaking to you personally through the testimony. Finally, for those who wish to dig deeper, there will be a *Selah Moments* reflection resource that will offer an opportunity to sit alone at the feet of Jesus and allow the Holy Spirit to wash your soul and renew your mind with the Word of God. Look for details at the end of the book for how to access this resource once it becomes available.

The Almighty, Living God of the universe has prepared a place of healing and restoration for you because He deems you worthy. Will you take His hand and let His love ignite your faith? Step forward in courage. A freedom you never thought possible awaits you.

> *Note: There are some vulnerable moments in my story that may be triggers for those who have experienced personal trauma or abuse. Please wisely and prayerfully consider your engagement with this story, and seek counsel or care if you find yourself triggered by any part of it.*

CHAPTER ONE

DADDY ISSUES

"Even if my mother or father forsake me, He will receive me."

Psalm 27:10 NIV

One of my first memories of my dad is a handsome, tall, athletic man with light brown hair and ocean blue-green, eyes coming home in a drunken rage and sending my mom flying down the stairs. When Dad was in the picture, our home was filled with chaos, anger, hurt, and insults. Snarky and unkind words were spewed over everyone about the smallest things.

We lived in a villa with a compartment under the stairs where I loved to escape. It was my little place where I could play with my toys, snuggle with my blankets and stuffed animals, and hide when I was scared. I would take our cute bunny, Thumper, in there with me and pretend to be his mama. Under the stairs in my little sanctuary, I promised to keep him safe from the chaos bouncing around the walls outside of my haven. Above me, I could always hear that creaking sound as people went up and down the stairs like an old Victorian home with rolling banisters.

But on one particular day, those subtle creaks turned into loud thumps, followed by screaming and crying. While I was playing under the stairs, my mom confronted my dad about abusing my older siblings. As I heard her tumbling down the stairs, my chest tightened. My head was dizzy. Streams of salt-laden tears soaked my face. My little arms were shaking as I clenched my stuffed animals so tightly, hoping they could protect me. I squeezed my eyes closed as hard as I could, wishing it was just a bad dream.

I had various repressed memories from this time in my childhood that would come out later in therapy. Many times, my sister would hide me under the bed to protect me while my dad abused her. We shared a room, and her innocence was stolen alongside my own. In the earliest and most formative years of my life, my father's brokenness would cut, damage, and open doors for the enemy to prey on my soul. The trauma would birth a ripple of dysfunction into my teenage and adulthood years. I would go on to experience anxiety, depression, low self-esteem, repressed anger, panic attacks, excessive attention seeking, sexual sin with both men and women, lack of trust in relationships, night terrors, a drive to achieve and perform to prove myself worthy, and manipulation of others to feel in control.

Daddy was supposed to *protect*. Daddy was supposed to *affirm*. Daddy was supposed to be *safe*. Daddy was supposed to *love*.

And yet I began to accept a lie that would become a destructive core belief in my life: "*Something must be wrong with you, Jaymee. If your own father treats you like this, then you must have no worth.*"

Unloved. Unprotected. *Unworthy*.

These lies were like a bomb cyclone dropped into my soul that flooded the next 22 years of my life with chaos and destruction. These lies would shape the lens through which I viewed myself, others, and even God. The truth is, we repeat what we don't repair. What is not transformed in one generation is transferred to the next. I did not know how to escape the damage caused by my father's rejection.

My mom tried to rescue us. She packed us up while my dad was at work, and we left that night, leaving behind Thumper, my stuffed animal babies, my secret hideout under the stairs, and everything except the clothes we could pack. We left behind everything we knew, but our souls were branded with deep wounds that would be with us for a lifetime.

We lived in a family friend's garage for a year, hiding from him.

My mom was 30 years old at the time. She was hospitalized because of the stress, but finally she was able to file for a divorce. After the divorce, my dad refused to let us go. I was in pre-school at this time, and he found out the location by following my mom one day. He came by the pre-school, showed his ID to prove he was my father, and he took me from the pre-school without my mom's knowledge. She was mortified when she came to pick me up after work to find out my dad had taken me. I don't really remember the details of how she was able to get me back. Mom doesn't like to talk about these times much, but I know we moved constantly for the next four years until he finally remarried and moved on.

It brings great insecurity and confusion to a young child when someone who is supposed to love and protect you becomes a danger to your well-being. My sister became suicidal and was constantly struggling with school and getting into fights. My brother got caught up in selling drugs and gang activity and watched his best friend get murdered. Trauma, abuse, and dysfunction created more chaos. My mom turned to busyness, other romantic relationships, and work to cope with the trail of pain my dad left in his wake. At one point, she took us to a church, looking for hope and help. They didn't say it directly, but it was clear that we didn't "fit" their congregation. A single, divorced mom, two teenagers that were in complete rebellion, and a little, dishwater brown-haired 8-year-old girl with bright blue eyes who was broken to the core looked like black sheep to this particular church community. Sadly, my mom gave up on God, too.

During my early childhood years, I remember constantly living in a state of *fear*. I never wanted to sleep alone. I remember sharing a bed with my older sister, Charity, who we called "Chewy" because it was easier to pronounce. I would demand Chewy to hold my hand super tight every single night so I could fall asleep.

The fear grew into every part of my life. I remember riding my bike to school and feeling afraid of getting kidnapped. I had nightmares regularly. I lived most of my early childhood in fight-or-flight mode due to the trauma. As I grew, I began to learn how to stuff away my fear and shift into a mode of achievement. I worked hard at school and every activity, because those were the only places where I felt any sense of control in my life. I saw how proud my mom was of me, and I soon became the golden child that did everything "right." My sister and brother put so much stress on my mom. I felt like I could ease her pain by being the "good" kid. This became my mission and motivation, because when mom was less stressed, everything was better.

During this time, I became very attached to my mom in an unhealthy way. I did not like it when she dated men. I was afraid they would hurt her, or us, and felt very uneasy about any man in her life. I would cry when she went on dates, and I never wanted to be around any of them. I had learned that men could not be trusted. I remember acting out with extreme anger if I sensed that she was becoming serious in her dating relationships. Little did I realize how these events in early childhood would set me up for great hardships and confusion in young adulthood when it came to romantic relationships.

When I was around ten years old, my mom connected with an old high school friend, Larry. Soon they would start dating, and eventually they got married. I actually felt safe with Larry as my stepdad. We moved to another city and became a blended family with Larry and his two kids. I was at peace with this transition, and these times were a breath of fresh air for my mom and me. My older siblings had moved out on their own, and some of my best childhood memories were built in my middle school and high school years. However, I had not found a healing relationship with Jesus yet, and it was only a matter of time before the stuffed-up trauma of my past would find its way into the mess.

One night when I was in 8th grade, we were awakened in the middle of the night with a loud knock at our door. We lived in a small town in the mountains of Colorado. Everybody knew everybody. I played sports with the police chief's daughter and so we had personal relationships with our local law enforcement. We knew any knock on the door in the middle of the night wasn't good.

It was the police visit every parent fears.

My older stepbrother, Adam, had been involved in a drinking and driving accident.

He was thrown from the car.

Everything happened so fast.

Crying, yelling, and weeping engulfed my mom and stepdad.

Everyone was in shock.

The next thing I knew I was riding in the car to the accident scene. There, covered up with a blanket, was the lifeless body of my brother.

This was my first experience of facing death.

Grief is hard no matter what. Children are not supposed to go before their parents. Yet, grieving in healthy ways is nearly impossible without a relationship with Jesus, and none of us had Jesus. He was there weeping with us, but we didn't know Him. We didn't know about His peace, His comfort, or how He could use something so horrible for our good if we would just reach for His hand.

We didn't know.

In the coming months, my stepdad Larry would fall into a deep depression. A few months later, he also lost his mom to natural causes. The sting of death was too much for the marriage, and they filed for divorce shortly thereafter. My mom and I had to leave and be on our own once again.

This was a lot of loss for a 14-year-old girl with buried trauma, as her broken heart endured the loss of her brother *and* another broken marriage that she internalized as rejection from another father figure. More daddy issues piled on. And the grief? Mom and I did what we always did: *stuff it and keep moving forward.* Mom had to figure out how to be a single mom again. I had goals to accomplish and dreams to chase. Nobody had time to grieve.

As I entered high school, I continued my crisis management protocol: I studied, I achieved, and I performed. And I did it very well. I was working hard to stay on the golden child pedestal I had been put on. It allowed me to feel a false sense of security and control when so much of my life had been out of control. During this time, I was very involved in sports: volleyball, basketball, and soccer. Our high school was a basketball powerhouse after winning three state championships in a row, and in our small town, sports were the life of the community. The stands were always packed, and everyone embraced our basketball program's success as their own. This is where I met the head coach for both the volleyball and basketball teams: Coach Benyo.

Coach Benyo was intense.

When you did well, everyone in the gym knew it.

When you did poorly, everyone in the gym knew it.

I thrived on his high expectations. He had the in-your-face-but-also-your-biggest-cheerleader approach to coaching. I loved structure and accountability. It felt secure. It felt like he cared.

He knew the game so well and had the championship rings to prove it. Over the next three years of playing for him,

I developed a bond with Coach B, as did many of his players. He was like another father figure to us, especially those of us without dads in our lives. He was a hard-core coach, but he was sincere in wanting the best for his players. He was also my biology teacher. He provided a space in my life where I felt seen, encouraged, and held accountable. He was a man that genuinely cared about my safety and my future, and he was always pushing me to do better in a loving way.

Coach Benyo was married with two kids, who I babysat a few times. He had team dinners with his family and really poured into his job as a coach. He was a dedicated husband, father, coach, and teacher, and I admired him.

My junior year, there was a group of us that had been playing basketball together since the 7th grade. We were a powerhouse squad of teammates and best friends who could dominate together on the basketball court. It was our year to bring back the state championship trophy! Everything was in alignment, and all of our hard work and dedication over the years was paying off.

Until another bomb dropped.

Through a series of conversations with school officials, it was disclosed that Coach Benyo had been having inappropriate interactions with one of his players. One of my *teammates*. The entire community was devastated. We cried in disbelief, anger, and hurt. The media went crazy, and even though there weren't any criminal charges filed, he lost everything. He packed up his family and moved to another state, and just like that, another "dad" was gone from my life.

For the third time in those most impressionable years, the father figures in my life left me feeling worthless, rejected, abused, or abandoned.

I was good at stuffing the pain, but what we stuff *stays*.
Nothing remains hidden forever.
Time does not heal all wounds.

I dated some throughout high school and began drinking and partying a lot to help me ignore the pain. I sought attention from young men, but never fully trusted them. I would uphold the good-girl image on the outside, but I felt a growing sense of rebellion. I remained a virgin until my senior year because I just didn't trust guys. The rejection narrative was rooted deeply. I believed that if my own dad couldn't love me, I didn't show much promise for a healthy romantic relationship.

What did a loving, humble, sacrificial, hard-working, safe man look like?

I didn't have a clue.

I wanted to be married and have kids one day, but the men in my life had proven to be very untrustworthy.

I ended up getting a college scholarship at the University of Tampa to play basketball, pursue a double major, and perform on the dance team. Full throttle in all the things. But it didn't take long until the next bomb dropped.

My freshmen semester, one of my roommates was raped at knife point. I was so done. Men were living up to the reputation I had always known. Selfish. Untrustworthy. Abusive. Dangerous. Using women for sex. The guys I did know that had serious relationships were cheating on their girlfriends or trying to hook up with other women. It made me sick. I was done with men.

This made it really easy for the enemy to lure me into a place that seemed "safer": a relationship with a woman. My best friend became my lover because even though I knew I wasn't a lesbian, she felt safe. Of course, when I opened this door, spiritually, it opened so many others.

Jealousy.
Confusion.
Relationship chaos.
Drama.
Emotional unrest.
Lust.

The enemy always uses our wounds and weaknesses to deceive us when it comes to what it means to love or be loved. God is love, but I did not have God in my life. I didn't have healthy examples of love from the men in my life. I was prime prey.

I know same-sex attraction is a touchy subject. There are many things going on spiritually with this dynamic, and I invite you to read more about this in the resource section of the *Selah Moments* devotional. For now, I will simply say this: God loves people who struggle with same-sex attraction just the same as the heterosexual who is addicted to porn or having sex outside of marriage. I know many Christians don't love this way, but God does. At the same time, the truth is that same-sex relationships are not God's plan for His creation. I know that might offend some, but only the truth can set us free. God's love is big enough to handle it.

I dated my female friend off and on for two years in college, but I was also constantly drawn back to men. It was a season of complete confusion on so many levels. I didn't know who I was sexually. I didn't know what I wanted, so I just rode a rollercoaster of allowing my feelings to dictate every decision. I put myself in situations that could have gone so wrong, if not for the grace of God.

In my senior year of college, I met my current husband. We will pick up on *that* story in chapters to come. However, there were years of dysfunction when it came to dating in my young adult years. My self-esteem and my identity were under a full-fledged attack, and the enemy was winning.

I was empty.
I was broken.
I was lost.

CHAPTER TWO

PERFECT PERFORMANCE

"For God has not given us a spirit of fear, but of power, and of love, and of a sound mind."

2 Timothy 1:7 NKJV

My heart sank as I smelled the stench of alcohol on his breath. I realized by his slurred speech that he had been drinking. My chest tightened with great sadness, and I had to hold back tears as they streamed down the back of my throat. This was the only basketball game my dad ever came to, and he came intoxicated. My cheeks burned with embarrassment. Soon, his cutting words would follow.

Even though my dad was addicted to alcohol, I still had a longing for his approval. After all, he was my dad. Most of the time he was what you would call a "functional" alcoholic. He would still go to work and seem to be productive, but it didn't take long to recognize the negative effects of his addiction. As a child, I would internalize this dysfunction as a need to earn his approval through achievement. He seemed to love me more when I performed well.

PERFECT PERFORMANCE

Perfectionism and performance-based worth are an attempt to cover up pain from being dismissed, devalued, abused, or overly criticized, especially by our parents. This was the essence of my motivation for most of my teen and young adulthood life: to earn his love and respect. Yet no matter how much I accomplished or how well I performed, my mind would inevitably be overwhelmed by the lingering voices of perfectionism and deep-rooted insecurity.

Not good enough.
Rejected.
Unloved.

I believed that no matter how well I performed or how "good" I acted, it wasn't enough. And I believed that I had to continually prove my worth. When I got straight A's, I got hugs, money, and praise from him. When I didn't measure up and got anything less, I received the piercing, critical words, "I am disappointed in you."

Or, sometimes, unspoken disapproval. He said nothing.

So, I achieved. I performed. I strived. I did it to run from the pain of rejection. I did it with the hope of being loved. All that time, what I truly needed was the love of Jesus, but I didn't know Him yet.

In 8th grade, I played on a competitive basketball team. I remember being so eager to play one particular game, because we were in the city where my dad lived, so that meant there was a chance he would come and see me play. I remember feeling so much joy when I saw him walk into that gym! He had never seen me play any sports and had never come to any of my dance performances. I played my tail off, diving after every ball. It was probably my best defensive game ever as I racked up steal after steal. I hit all my free throws. Throughout the game, I kept track of all the stats in my head, confident that I had *performed* well. After the game, I ran up to my dad to give him the biggest hug. Like a puppy awaiting approval from his owner, I anticipated the approval I so desperately craved.

And then I saw it. I smelled it. He was drunk, eyes glossy, and the fermented scent of beer lingered on his breath.

And then he spoke. "I thought you were a better player than what I saw today."

Now, if my dad had been in my life regularly and shown love at different opportunities, that critique probably would not have cut so deep. I was already bleeding from all the hits I had taken over time, and this was throwing salt at the gaping wound in my heart. The power of a parent's words can bring life or death. All I wanted was to know I was loved.

I thought, on this day, maybe I had earned it.

Instead, every word out of his mouth was critical. He pointed out every single thing I did wrong, and what I could have done better. Not a single word of edification or encouragement. I heard other dads cheering for their daughters and praising them from the stands. I just wanted to know my dad was *for me*. I wanted to know that he was proud to be my dad no matter what. I wanted to know he believed in me.

Instead, more pain. More rejection.

Anger exploded through me, and I felt like a bursting thermometer. My hopes of being seen, loved, and affirmed collapsed like a building in an earthquake. My heart quivered into a pile of rubble, and emptiness was all I could find in the aftermath. The lies echoed, *"Jaymee, you just aren't good enough. You will never be good enough."*

My dad was a wrecking ball to my self-worth. He pummeled my heart, destroying it piece by piece. The abuse, the rejection, the criticism, the negativity, the neglect, and the abandonment just compounded the lie: *I am not worthy.* So up the walls went around my heart. I would make a vow to never let the pain he caused stop me from being successful. I would protect my heart at all costs.

I was going to prove him wrong. I was going to achieve, perform, and become everything he thought I wasn't. Then maybe, just maybe…he would love me, he would accept me, and he would think I was worthy.

If I achieved enough, the pain would stop.

These were lies upon lies, but the lies were loud. The core lie behind all of it was simply this: *For me to be worthy and valuable, I must do more, achieve more, become more, work more, and I must do it perfectly.*

Just perform. Just achieve. Just excel. Then you will be loved, then you will be accepted, then you will be valuable. Then you will prove to everyone who rejected or dismissed you they were wrong. It was another trap of warped thinking and wrong motivation, a false narrative stealing space in my head. And it consumed me.

You know what's crazy? We all know perfection is not a reality. We know we are human, and we have weaknesses. We know at some point in life we have failed or will experience failure. So why do we so often find ourselves buying into this perfectionist mentality?

Perfectionism is not a desire to be perfect, but it's a desire to FEEL perfect.

It's like a dopamine hit for us every time we achieve, perform, and do something well. It temporarily numbs the pain of our true brokenness and insecurity. In those moments of victory, we get to say, *"I feel worthy. I feel seen. I feel good enough."*

During times when I was feeling "less than," I would begin to immaculately clean everything, organize like nobody's business, nail a killer work-out, get my hair redone, buy a new outfit; anything that would make me feel like I was winning. In today's culture, I would have probably posted about all these things on social media, seeking the applause of people, convinced that if everyone else said I was worthy, then I must be.

Needing the validation of people can be addictive. We can't handle the feeling of failure or rejection, so we seek how to achieve our next "high." We post something that gets tons of likes and views with the perfect filter, lighting, pose, and caption. We sign up for a gazillion things at our kid's school or at work or church and wear "busyness" like a badge of honor. We put more job titles and achievements in our social media bios to tell the world how much we have accomplished to somehow elevate our social status in the eyes of others.

Yet for most of us, this is insecurity at its finest. And if it's not insecurity, it's a glorification of self rather than glorifying God.

Here's what I have learned: that momentary feeling of "nailing it" is short-lived. Life brings more rejection and failure. And the cycle starts all over again. Most of us performance-based people also struggle with the comparison trap. Instead of embracing how God made us and the gifts He gave us, we conclude we are not enough.

I remember the waves of discontentment and comparison that would overtake me during those years.

"Why do they get those blessings?"
"Why do I have it so hard?"
"Why is their life so easy?"
"Why is my life like this?"

It was a combination of insecurity, complaining, and a lack of gratitude. I didn't embrace God's plan for me, and I certainly didn't see the mess I made by *my own choices*. Free will is real, and so are the consequences of our choices.

Instead of self-reflection, envy linked arms with my guilt, self-condemnation, and unworthiness. The vicious cycle continued: insecurity, offense, defensiveness, gossip, jealousy.

How did I battle all these negative feelings?

Do more.

Accomplish more.

Excel more.

Then wait for the applause.

Hope that through this I would be worthy to be loved.

This was not God's plan for my life.

This cycle was my coping mechanism for years. All the trauma, all the struggles, all the internal turmoil. Cope. Conceal. Strive. Even if I didn't have it all together, I sure was going to convince you that I did. I was strong, and I didn't need anyone else's help. I just got things done. People would admire me for my accomplishments and strength. This was the goal.

Since I was a very little girl, the quest for acceptance and admiration through accomplishment permeated my entire life.

I was

The straight-A student.

The homecoming queen.

The basketball team captain.

The student body president.

The dance team choreographer.

The MVP in multiple sports.

The kids' camp volunteer.

The exercise addict.

The double major in college.

The Teacher of the Year.

The Coach of the Year.

The mom who made every bit of food from scratch and kept a "perfect" sleep schedule and food log for my babies.

The teenager who would get up and reorganize my entire room in the middle of the night.

The college student who color-coordinated her closet perfectly.

The keeper of the perfect house, with everything in its perfect place.

The fitness instructor and collegiate athlete obsessed with her looks and body.

We perfectionist types many times operate from a place of wanting to control. For me, my emotions and soul were out of control, but performing, achieving, and attempting to do it perfectly made me feel in control.

But I wasn't.

Don't get me wrong, many of the things we all do are great things. I believe we should do everything God has entrusted us to do with excellence. But what I couldn't see for so many years was the motivation behind my striving. I wasn't working to glorify God. I was working to glorify myself. I was working to cover up my pain.

And why? What was my motive? Vanity? Pride? Jealousy? People's approval? Insecurity? Pain? A need to be seen? To be validated? Perhaps it was all of those things, but in all honestly, when it comes down to it, one of the driving forces behind my desire to be in control is *fear*.

Fear of failure. Fear of rejection. Fear of making mistakes. Fear of the opinions of others. Fear of succeeding. Fear of disappointing people.

I still struggle in this area at times, and I have to check myself. Why am I using a filter that hides my wrinkles? Why do I choose to wear black yoga pants 6 days a week just to feel "slimmer" because perimenopause has been rough, and I'm not comfortable in my own skin? Why do I still sometimes desire applause from people rather than from heaven? Even writing this book, why do I find myself re-reading the chapters over and over as I write, wanting them to be "perfect"?

The struggle is real.

I am still a work in progress.

Fear and pride toss us back and forth like a pendulum.

God has a new narrative He wants us to embrace:

> *"For God has not given us a spirit of fear, but of power and of love of a sound mind."*
>
> **2 Timothy 1:7**

Fear is from the enemy of our souls, not from God. It is a snare that keeps us from walking in peace, freedom, and all that God has planned for us. Fear is sneaky and subtle at times. But I have experienced a different way. God's spirit, the Holy Spirit, gives us power over fear. His love and presence cast out fear. If we want to have a self-disciplined and sound mind, we must kick fear out of our thoughts. The fearful thoughts may come, but we have a choice whether to listen to them or not.

I have discovered that nothing will keep us further away from the will of God for our lives than being afraid of what other people think of us. I cannot follow Jesus and seek validation from man at the same time. People pleasing, choosing to compromise my values, bowing to peer pressure, striving for perfection, and all of the rest of my fear-based choices never actually proved my worthiness.

God saw right through my pretending. God did not need my perfect performance. He wanted my full heart and full surrender. He wanted my repentance, for me to turn away from doing things *my way*. He wanted to heal me and set me free from my fear. He wanted me to know that I am loved beyond measure, despite my flaws, wounds, and failures.

> *"Can anything ever separate us from Christ's love? Does it mean he no longer loves us if we have trouble, calamity, or are persecuted, or hungry, or destitute, or in danger, or*

threatened with death? As it is written: 'For your sake we face death all day long; we are considered as sheep to be slaughtered.' No, in all these things we are more than conquerors through Him who loved us. For I am convinced that neither death nor life, neither angels nor demons, neither the present nor the future, nor any powers, neither height nor depth nor anything else in all creation, will be able to separate us from the love of God that is in Christ Jesus our Lord."

Romans 8:35-39 NLT

Through the many painful chapters of my life, I have learned the truth of this passage of scripture. Every day, it becomes more real and more powerful. Nothing and no one can separate us from the love of Jesus Christ. Jesus is enough. No one's opinion of us matters but His.

Our purpose for living is not about being perfect, having the biggest bank account, the hottest spouse, the newest car, the nicest body, the largest platform, or the most followers on social media. It's not about who went to the best college, or who has the most achievements, trophies, and titles. This is the world's definition of success. These can be places of influence, but they are not our identities. They don't determine our worth as human beings.

My life is not all about me. My life is about what Jesus can do through me for His glory alone. Instead of seeking perfection or achieving to be valuable, I choose to seek *confident humility*.

I choose to be confident because I know who I belong to, but I must remain humble enough to know I am nothing without Him, and I can do nothing of eternal value without Him.

I wish I could have learned this truth about my worth and value in the early years of my life. I wish someone would have shared the truth about God and authentic relationship with Jesus Christ. I wish I would have known and understood the depth of love that He has for me. Instead, I was set on a relentless path to achieve, to strive, and to prove myself. I believed that if I did enough, I might finally be worthy of love. It would take a series of failures, wounds, heartaches, and traumas before my heart would be ready to receive God's truth that I was worthy simply because He created me and valued me.

The next chapter of my story nearly destroyed me. Driven by fear, pride, and a desperate need to be loved, I made choices that now live in the quiet corners of my memory as some of my deepest regrets. God redeems, forgives, and heals, but this particular journey of suffering was not His will for my life.

CHAPTER THREE

SHAMEFUL SECRETS

> *"Instead of shame, you will receive a double portion, and instead of disgrace, you will rejoice in your inheritance. And so you will inherit a double portion in your land, and everlasting joy will be yours."*
>
> **Isaiah 61:7 NIV**

My boyfriend wasn't ready for marriage, and the fear of raising a child alone made getting an abortion seem like the right thing to do. At 25 years old, I was teaching full-time while also working on my master's degree, instructing fitness classes, and coaching a girls' basketball team.

My life was comfortable and going just as I planned. I couldn't wait to get married and start a family, but marriage was not on my boyfriend's radar. We were "playing house," pretending to be husband and wife, but neither of us were mature enough to follow God's design for relationships and marriage. We were coasting through life, living how we wanted, claiming to be Christians because we believed in God, but we had no relationship with Jesus. Selfishness, fear of commitment, convenience, and all the rationalizations to do things "our way" had led us to this point. When I told my boyfriend the news that I was pregnant, he seemed completely indifferent.

Here we go again.

That obnoxious, loud voice of rejection began to infiltrate all my thoughts. *"He doesn't want you or the baby, Jaymee,"* the voice taunted.

My mind and heart were instantly bombarded with fear and all the "what if" scenarios. *What if I am an unwed mother? What will people think? How will I raise this baby alone? How can I afford to do this on my own? I don't want to raise my kids in a broken home like mine. I can't do this alone. My boyfriend doesn't want to marry me, so what would that look like if we have this baby? Would he leave me and take the baby? Would he abandon me?*

I would cry myself to sleep every night as these thoughts tormented me. My mind raced like a freight train. My heart pounded like a galloping horse.

Ever since I was a little girl, I couldn't wait to be a mom. I loved being "the mom" and playing with all my stuffed animals, teaching them, taking care of them, and singing to them. I had made a vow that I would never even consider having an abortion because I knew that my dad had wanted to abort me. The idea of asking my mom to abort me seemed like a sensible solution to my dad, too. He was 40 years old, and they already had 4 kids between the two of them. His fears of having another mouth to feed and starting over with an infant at his age made having an abortion seem like a simple fix.

When I first heard about this as an adult, I thought, *"How could my dad not want me?"* and even worse, *"Did my dad want to have me killed?"*

I have to be honest that even though I have forgiven my dad, this wound stings more than any other. Daddy was supposed to be the one who *protected me*. It was another round of rejection, abandonment, and selfishness, and this one was hard to get past. The weight of knowing I was unwanted by one of my parents still doesn't sit gently in my heart or mind. I know my dad was lost and broken, but those truths don't take away the internal turmoil or the damage done.

It's easy to sit and say, "*I would never...*" about anything. Yet I have learned in my 48 years of life, the moment a prideful statement like that is made, many of us find ourselves doing the very things we never thought we would do. If we are honest, we all have hypocrisy intertwined somewhere in our story.

So here comes one of the most hypocritical decisions of my life.

I would decide to kill my innocent baby.

Fear is relentless.
Fear paralyzes.
Fear torments.
Fear is a liar.
Fear is from the pit of hell.

The fear narrative that repeated in my head was very convincing. Like a tsunami, it flooded my mind and pushed my emotions to all kinds of irrational places. I took the bait, I listened to the wrong voice, and I got trapped in the snare of fear. My boyfriend and I went to the Yellow Pages and found a clinic that would administer the abortion pill. I made the appointment over spring break so I could have an excuse to not work or teach classes. At five weeks along, there didn't seem to be any health risks, *so we were told.*

The drive to the clinic seemed like an eternity and we were silent the whole way there. Finally, we arrived and parked the car. As we were walking to the door of the clinic, I'll never forget what happened. It seemed like God sent a divine intervention right at that moment, an angel in flesh. As I reached for the doorknob, a light-haired woman in her late 40s wearing all white and a cross necklace approached me and put her hand ever-so-gently on my arm. She kindly pleaded, "Please don't do this." Her eyes were loving and sincere.

The pit in my stomach sank deeper. I choked back all the tears that were trying to burst forth, but my mind was already in bondage as the enemy whispered, *"You have to do this."*

I side-stepped her, and my boyfriend opened the door. We walked into the clinic, a place of fear and death. I was extremely nervous and scared. My body was cold, my palms were sweaty, and my heart was racing a mile a minute. I felt nauseous and my head was pounding. The lobby was full, but I didn't pay attention to anyone else because I was so caught up in my own emotions. With my hands shaking, I signed in, filled out the paperwork, and waited for the nurse to call me. My boyfriend held my hand with a death grip. He was trying to be tough and strong, but I could tell he was scared, too.

The nurse began to take my vitals, but I felt faint and weak. She said that I looked pale. I remember her taking my blood pressure and it being ridiculously low. Moments later, I started hyperventilating and losing consciousness. I was having an anxiety attack. Trembling, I could not catch my breath. My chest caved in, like a ton of bricks were pressing down as I gasped for air.

The nurse pushed a brown bag into my face as I struggled for each breath.

When she finally got me stabilized, she directed me to a "counseling session". When I look back on it now, my heart breaks at how every person on staff at the clinic was so desensitized to the killing of innocent children. The counseling session was more of an opportunity for them to convince me that the choice I made was "normal," "safe," and "not a big deal."

After counseling, they did a sonogram to confirm I was pregnant. I also remember that they never showed me the sonogram. I'm sure if I saw my baby, it would have connected to some place deep in my heart and begged me to change my mind.

Oh, how I wish I would have changed my mind.

They gave me the abortion pill.
I swallowed it.

I felt part of my soul being shattered into 1000 pieces. The permanence of death was in that one gulp, and destruction began to take place inside my body. Nobody can ever prepare you for what you experience when you abort your baby. God created women uniquely to create life, not take it. As a mom of a daughter, I can never imagine my sweet girl ever experiencing the trauma this choice brought to my life. Abortion is not just the removal of pregnancy tissue or a clump of cells. Abortion is the ending of a human life.

They gave me a prescription for pain and sent us on our way like it was a drive-through restaurant.

The lady at the front desk called out the next woman's name.

On the way home, I silently wept as I tried to hold in all the emotional pain. I had always been taught that abortion was the woman's choice, and that since it was so early in the pregnancy, it wasn't a baby. Yet, in the depths of my soul, I heard an inner voice saying that this was *all wrong*.

My boyfriend filled the pain med prescription for me. The nurses had said the pain would be "similar to strong menstrual cramps." Well, that was a big fat lie. A few hours later, I was in the fetal position, screaming and crying in the most intense pain I had ever felt. For the entire night I wept, bled, and wailed through the experience of life being ripped from my womb on my hallway floor. I was sure I was dying physically, mentally, and most definitely spiritually. Lost and afraid, my boyfriend lay beside me, helplessly weeping with me.

I would find out years later that he had always wanted to keep the baby, but had been taught that it was the woman's choice. This is why he appeared indifferent when I first shared the news. He had been told he was powerless and that his voice didn't matter. "Her body, her choice." Men experience grief and consequences of this choice as well. God created women to carry life, but life is formed by the union of both man and woman. That child was his child as well.

The pain was so intense that everything was a big blur for eight to ten hours. For three more days, I was in agony, and the bleeding would not stop. I thought I was surely going to die. Finally, I called the clinic, and they concluded that the entire fetus had not been aborted. They would have to go in and surgically remove the rest. I was mortified, because I thought it would be less invasive to just "take a pill." I sobbed for hours and hours. I can only imagine the tears Jesus was shedding for me in those moments. I know he was weeping for me, my boyfriend, and *my baby girl*.

I could barely walk back into the same clinic I had wanted to run away from. In those moments, I just wanted to die to be free from all the pain. Clenching my abdomen, whimpering loudly, I stumbled into the room where they would perform the procedure. The smell of death filled the air.

I woke up screeching at the top of my lungs and was met with the doctor and nurse holding me down and angrily yelling at me since I was "scaring the other patients."

Sobbing.
Staggering.
Broken.

Like a ragdoll, I made my way back out of the clinic and slid into my boyfriend's car. I thought the anguish was finally over. But the consequences of that decision had only begun to wreak their havoc on my life. The narrative of rejection was reinforced with excruciating certainty. The little girl under the stairs with all her trauma was growing up believing she was unwanted and unworthy, like she always feared.

My 25-year-old self was longing in every way to be accepted and loved. The voice of unworthiness and rejection whispered into her mind regularly. In her mind, the voice of rejection confirmed her unworthiness when the boyfriend didn't respond with, "Let's get married. Let's have this baby together. We can do this." Instead, she was met with, "I will support you in whatever *you decide.*"

To her, that response was that same voice again, *"Nobody wants you, Jaymee. You are not worthy enough. He doesn't even care."*

The enemy was showing me more *proof and evidence* that I was rejected. Unwanted. Unworthy.

And so, I believed him.

I believed so many lies.

Lies of fear.

Lies that my baby was "just a blob of tissue."

Lies that it was just a "medical procedure."

The list of lies went on and on.

And in the wake of these lies, in the shadow of the choice I made, shame seized the center stage of my story. I had broken a deep, internal vow. All I wanted was to be a mom one day. How could I ever think about having an abortion when my dad wanted to abort me? Yet there I was, doing the very thing I promised myself I would never do.

The enemy drew me in with pride, selfishness, and fear so that I would cave to his will. He convinced me that the wrong thing was the right thing. Then, after I listened, he nailed me with shame, condemnation, and unworthiness. Shame is a weapon that he has sharpened and perfected, one that will destroy relationships, subvert healing, steal hope, and corrode peace.

Shame says *if I did something bad, that means I am bad.*
Shame says *I will be broken forever and that I cannot be fixed.*
Shame says *I can never change.*

Shame says *I have to hide all my secrets so I don't show my weakness.*

Shame says *if something bad is done to me, I am bad and worthless.*

SHAME LIES. These are ALL LIES.

Shame says that I can never tell anyone because then people will know the real me, and they will judge me. Shame wants me to be isolated. Shame wants me to suffer alone. Shame wants to keep everything in the dark.

Shame ate me alive for years.
Oh, how I wish I had known Jesus back then.
I desperately needed His love, healing, truth, and comfort during those dark times.

Jesus redeems all. He wants to redeem all the shameful secrets that we keep hidden. Shame can't heal until it is brought into the light. Shame hides the secrets we deeply regret, secrets we would never tell a soul. Failure, sin, and guilt that bring so much embarrassment and shame we can't even say them out loud are silenced by our shame. And in the silence, we suffer.

The shame of my abortion consumed me.
It was a failure.
It was sinful.
It was regretful.
It was agony.

Yet there is a power far greater than my shame. There is a love that crushes every fear. There is hope and healing that tramples the condemnation and the lie of unworthiness. Jesus heals our broken hearts. He loves us no matter what we have done. He shows us that we are worthy to be loved and that we are loved. Once we come into a relationship with Jesus and repent, He forgives us for everything we have ever done. But we have to admit and acknowledge all of it to Him.

Today, the truth about the shame of my abortion is that it is wiped away.

I am healed.
I am redeemed.
I am forgiven.
The old is gone and the new has come.

I can't go back and change that regretful decision, but I have chosen to heal with Jesus. I chose to take post-abortion healing classes in a community of other women who had made the same decision. I chose to write a book to share my story. I have chosen to honor her life.

Jennale, how Mommy loves you so much. I am so sorry that I chose to let you go. You would be 23 years old at the time I am writing this book. I wish I could have held you. I wish I could have felt your tiny hands holding mine. Every day, I hold tightly to God's promise to see you in heaven again one day! What a glorious day that will be. It brings me peace to know that you are with Jesus. It brings me comfort to know we will spend eternity together. At the same time, I hold the sting of your death in my soul. What life would you have led on earth? What impact could you have made?

I can choose not to wallow in regret, guilt, or allow the enemy to beat me up for that choice. I can encourage other women who have made that choice to bring it to the feet of Jesus. I can encourage other women who face an unplanned pregnancy to be courageous and keep the baby. I can stand firm knowing that God forgives me, and I can also *forgive myself*.

But before I experienced this healing with Jesus, I would have to go through greater struggle. I would make choices that would exponentially increase my shame. I would be publicly humiliated, punished, and scorned for those choices. I would see the devastating consequences of a life built on the lie of unworthiness. Here's the good news about the next painful, embarrassing, and shameful parts of my story: none of it was too big for God. From the ashes of my imminent demise, hope would arise.

> *"No measure of sin in your past life can deprive you of this promise....*
> *'Whosoever believeth on him shall not be ashamed.'"*[1]
> **- Charles H. Spurgeon**

---

[1] Daniels, J. (2020, March 13). *9 Spurgeon quotes on shame*. The Spurgeon Center.
https://www.spurgeon.org/resource-library/blog-entries/9-spurgeon-quotes-on-shame/

CHAPTER FOUR

I'M FINE, EVERYTHING IS FINE

"But he said to me, 'My grace is sufficient for you, for my power is made perfect in weakness.' Therefore, I will boast all the more gladly about my weaknesses, so that Christ's power may rest on me."

2 Corinthians 12:9 NIV

After the abortion, my boyfriend and I never talked about it. I couldn't even say the word "abortion." We would refer to it as a "procedure" or "miscarriage." It wasn't until I went through post-abortion counseling seven years later that I was able to even admit to it.

The week after the abortion, my boyfriend proposed to me. He felt the magnitude and fear of potential loss as we faced the reality that I could have died. He realized that his fear of commitment was not stronger than his fear of losing me. Later in counseling, he would share that he had wanted to keep the baby but had been taught it was not his choice. His fear and my rejection issues were the perfect recipe for the enemy to manipulate us both.

His proposal was what I always wanted. I wanted to marry him and start a family. However, after two and a half years together, I felt like he was getting all the benefits of a wife without the commitment. I didn't want to be with someone for years and not get married. I was in love with him, but I was ready to move to the next level. Up to that point, he was not. Before I found out that I was pregnant, I was considering moving out so he could figure out what he wanted.

Looking back on it now, through the perspective of God's design for marriage, I understand why moving in together before marriage is not God's plan. Women tend to think moving in together will bring the relationship closer to marriage and commitment. In contrast, most men admit that moving in together before marriage is about making it easier to have sex and for financial reasons. It's taking the easy road without commitment, without the protection of covenant.

We are all born selfish. We want to choose what's easy, what's most comfortable, and what satisfies us. We justify and rationalize our sin, but God sets boundaries and parameters for our relationships because *they are good for us*. When we decide to do things our way instead of God's, we will face consequences at some point.

These years were surrounded with consequences as we tried to undo the wrong ordering of our relationship. I did marry Craig. I did love him. I did want a family with him. But our marriage started with all the wrong foundations: selfishness, sexual sin, unresolved trauma, shame, and insecurity. It didn't take long for things to go wrong. I realized years later in therapy that I had built up resentment and anger. I blamed my husband for the abortion.

"If he had only stepped up like a man and asked me to marry him before the abortion, I would never have killed my baby. I almost died, our baby is dead, and *now he wants to marry me?! Why now?"*

These statements would echo through my mind for months. Confusion saturated my soul. I experienced this internal wrestling between relief that he wanted to marry me and a deep anger at his timing and cowardice. In addition, I felt emotionally neglected by Craig during this season. He was running from his pain in the situation through work and coaching. He was rarely home, and I once again felt abandoned emotionally.

I chose to bury the pain. I swept it under the rug and kept moving like nothing ever happened. I built walls around my heart so I didn't have to feel the anger. I convinced myself that I was strong, and that things would get better. *I just needed to keep going and move forward.*

Eventually, everything we stuff away, hide, or build walls around resurfaces. When we have not brought the pain to God and done the intentional deep work of healing, unprocessed pain will raise its ugly head through a plethora of dysfunctional behaviors. Warning signals in my soul were going off like a fire alarm: anger, depression, anxiety, rage, bitterness, fear, a desire to control others, jealousy, and suicidal thoughts. I justified them, buried them, and just kept telling myself, *"I'm fine. Everything is fine."*

Picture a decrepit ceiling with an attic door. The ceiling's surface is drooping, cracked, and turning a yellowish-brown tint. It looks unstable and soggy from years of mold, leaks, and wear and tear. My whole life I had been stuffing my pain, trauma, and sin in that attic. I could put together a good act on the outside with all those performance-based achievements. Yet, the abortion broke me. Everything in my attic came crashing down all at once.

I was drowning in emotional and mental anguish.
What I needed was a Savior.
What I needed was inner healing.
What I needed was to surrender and admit I was broken and that I could not fix myself.

I also needed to realize that *my boyfriend was not my savior*. We have a natural tendency to make our spouse or significant other into gods of sorts. We give away the power to define our worth and value to other humans who were never intended to hold such power. That's what I did with Craig. The expectations I had placed on him were not obtainable. I wanted him to save me, to heal me, to love me in a way that convinced me once and for all that I was worth it. I expected him to pick up the mess of my collapsed attic and put me back together again. Of course, he could do none of those things. No man could. Only the God who created us is capable of such healing.

I have watched so many people allow relationships to pull them right out of God's will for their lives. This always leads to paths of pain, and then we often blame God for the suffering we have caused. Like me, many of us jump from one relationship to another, or from one marriage to another, thinking the issue is the other person. Repeated patterns show us we have not dealt with our attic of sin or unhealed wounds.

We run to everyone and everything to ease the pain or seek love, but Jesus is who we truly need.

Craig was not meant to complete me as my husband, instead he was meant to complement me. Jesus is the only one that can make me whole. So many of us mistake lust for love and run right into sexual immorality. We fall into the trap of codependency and enabling, thinking that by "fixing" our partner, we're somehow making ourselves more valuable. We endure all kinds of toxic relationships out of what we call "love". But this is not love at all. It's a broken, distorted version of love, an insecure counterfeit of what God's definition of love was meant to be.

God is love. God created love, therefore God defines love. I've heard people say, "I love you," but it's really, "I lust for you." "I enable you." "I need to control you." "I want you for what you can do for me." These perspectives are selfish, and authentic love is not selfish.

I put unrealistic demands on Craig as my boyfriend and was expecting him to emotionally support me in a way only Jesus could. This was a crossroads moment for me. One path could lead to Jesus: His pure love, His healing, His forgiveness, His hope. The other path was rebellion, despair, destruction, and more suffering. Oh, what a choice I had to make.

The sad part is I didn't even know about Jesus or the weight of these choices in these moments. God was trying to get my attention, but I didn't even know He was pursuing me. I refused to admit my weakness, and I was blinded by my sin.

I kept pretending.

I doubled down in my own strength.

I didn't do anything that would bring me closer to God or closer to healing.

I didn't go to counseling.

I wasn't honest with Craig about my anger.

I hid everything that caused me to feel shame.

I was self-reliant.

I was self-sufficient.

I made friends with pride. We were two peas in a pod. We were besties taking selfies together daily. And we knew how to hide and *appear good*. We put on a great show for everyone around us. Pride loves the perfectionist, achiever type. Pride hates appearing weak. Pride refuses to admit brokenness.

Pride kept me believing the lie that I was strong enough, that I could be self-sufficient. I was an independent woman handling my business. I was fine. Everything was fine. Yet that voice of shame came to me daily to remind me of my unworthiness. What would anyone think of me if they knew the truth? What would people say about me if they knew the *real me?*

Pride said, *"You can't let anyone know the truth. You must always keep up this illusion that you have it all together."*

"Pride goes before destruction, a haughty spirit before a fall."

Proverbs 16:18 NIV

Over the next three years, I would make decision after decision that would bring disgrace, torment, and the greatest fall of my life. I would allow the spirit of pride to use me as a vessel of destruction like a tornado, devastating me and many important people in my life.

Pride is the ultimate prison.

It's well-decorated on the outside.

Beautiful flowers dangle from the ceiling of the cell.

Ornate details of style and presentation make the door look oh-so-inviting.

A fresh aroma like a candle diffuses through it in an attempt to mask the stench.

I thought I was free because everything looked so perfect and in place. *"I've got it all together. I'm so strong. My life looks amazing to anyone who stops to notice."* Yet that malodorous smell was hidden in the walls of that cell, like something rotten behind the drywall and concrete. I ignored it, I tried to cover it up, but the stench lingered behind the walls despite my efforts to pretend it wasn't there.

My drywall was thick, and I didn't know how to tear it down. I spent my whole life stuffing my pain and my sin away. Pride told me I was strong enough to get through this abortion crisis with self-sufficiency and my own strength. I was not going to give in to the weakness.

"I was fine. Everything would be fine. Just give it time, Jaymee."

I tried to silence the weakness and the emotions that come with it, but the negative thought train came barreling through my mind day after day. Especially at night. Every night, I would experience racing thoughts, a racing heart, and unrest. Then I subtly began to pull further away from the ones I loved, with an excuse of busyness so I didn't have to slow down enough to feel what I really felt.

Despair and hopelessness started to set in. I would relive the abortion events and suffer PTSD night after night. I would awaken sweating and screaming through my night terrors. I couldn't sleep. I couldn't eat. Depression began to consume me like a heavy, suffocating cloud. There would be days I pictured driving my car into a tree going as fast as I could just to end it all. My life didn't matter anymore. I just wanted the emotional torment to stop. Weeping, I would sit in my closet staring at my wrist with a knife. Maybe a few cuts would quiet the pain for a little while.

I could never do it. I would hold the knife pressed against my skin, violently shaking. Ugly crying, with snot smothering my face.

Somehow, a power greater than my desire to die would overtake me. I didn't know Jesus then, but He was there with me in that closet just the same. He was praying for me, and He was the one whispering to my soul, *"Jaymee, don't do this, please don't do this."*

I imagine His tears flooding the closet right along with mine.

The seduction of suicidal thoughts can be so intense. You begin to be persuaded that not only would the pain go away, but everyone else in your life would be better off without you. The enemy speaks his lies over you, assuring you that death is the solution. He pretends to be the voice of hope within the darkness and despair. *But it is all lies.*

The father of lies was whispering lie after lie into my thoughts. This is Satan's primary tactic against God's precious image bearers. He is the destroyer, and his number one goal was to take me out. Satan perverts, twists, and distorts the truth until we hate ourselves and make God the villain.

> *"God doesn't love you, Jaymee."*
> *"God doesn't care about you, Jaymee."*
> *"Where is God now, Jaymee?"*
> *"Your life doesn't matter, Jaymee."*
> *"Do you really think anything is going to get better, Jaymee?"*

My pride had led me to the brink of death itself. I was sucked into the lie of self-pity, powerlessness, and believing I had no purpose. Ending it all felt like the easiest solution, but I couldn't bring myself to it.

Thank God.

He hears our cries.

He wants to redeem every bad thing we have done or been through.

This is a promise when we choose Jesus.

He is not done with us.

In this world, we will have pain and suffering until the day we are called back to our original home: heaven. God doesn't promise a trouble-free life, but He promises to never leave us and never forsake us. He promises to walk through the fire with us. He promises to carry us when we cannot walk and to be our strength and our refuge. He promises to take everything that was meant to destroy us and use it for our good and the good of others.

I had people who identified themselves as Christians all around me, but no one ever invited me to church, and no one ever tried to share the gospel with me. The "Christians" around me never shared the truth. Even still, God tried to get my attention so many times. He gave me so many chances to seek Him, but I didn't listen. He wasn't going to force me to choose Him. The peace, hope, joy, and healing we desire can come no other way than through a personal relationship with Jesus Christ. Choosing Jesus activates the promises of God in our lives. But choosing Him means we must decide to turn away from our way of living. It's not Jesus *plus* my will; it's Jesus and only His will be done.

In my darkest days of considering suicide, I didn't know the truth about God's promises. And while I couldn't go through with my imagined scenarios of death, I couldn't find my way back to life.

I was not fine.

Everything was not fine.

And soon, my path would continue to devolve into more chaos.

> *"Pride is spiritual cancer: It eats up the very possibility of love, contentment, and even common sense."*[2]
>
> **- C.S. Lewis.**

---

[2] Lewis, C. S. (2001). *Mere Christianity*. HarperOne, p. 63.

CHAPTER FIVE

SPIRALING INTO THE MUD

"Then I will sprinkle clean water on you, and you shall be clean; I will cleanse you from all your filthiness and from all your idols."

Ezekiel 36:25 NKJV

A great loneliness began to consume me after the abortion and then the engagement. I threw myself into my work and hobbies, and so did my fiancé. I was around people all the time, but I was deeply lonely. Anger and resentment had taken root and began to surge through my mind and body. I had a warped expectation that somehow my fiancé was supposed to fix my brokenness. If he would just be home more, and do all the things I wanted him to, then surely I would be better. We just needed to go on more dates, have more sex, and spend more time together. Then I would feel better. I wanted Craig to be my savior and to fill the emptiness I felt.

I had spent most of my life up to this point seeking relationships and connections with people so I could feel better about myself and whatever would make me happy in the moment. I kept running to people instead of to God. I was putting the responsibility of my behavior or feelings on someone else. Relationships were meant to complement me, but never to fulfill me the way Jesus could.

Since Craig couldn't love me in a way that would fix all of my brokenness, I turned elsewhere.

I bowed down to false gods and then wondered why eventually I became worse than when I started. I felt relief temporarily, but the emptiness always returned. I worshipped the created things rather than the Creator, and this turned my heart away from God rather than towards Him.

With a calloused heart, I started stewing over all the wrongful things that had been done to me. I allowed it to consume my thoughts. Angry, frustrated, bitter, resentful, offended; I was lathered in all the negative thoughts and emotions. It was easier to deflect and blame than it was to reflect on my choices. After all, that's the way it started in the Garden. Adam blamed Eve, and Eve blamed the snake. We don't have a great track record as a human race of taking personal responsibility for our own choices.

I didn't even take time to self-reflect. Why am I acting this way? Why am I feeling this way? What is my sin that is causing more problems? What offense do I need to forgive? Is what I am thinking and doing rational? What are the lies I am believing about God, myself, my circumstance, or the person who hurt me?

I had isolated so far from any sort of help that I didn't know to ask these questions. Dripping in self-pity, I believed the lie that my healing was contingent on what others did or didn't do. It was a victim mentality. Painful, yet convenient, because it gave me an excuse to stay in the same broken spot. I didn't understand the magnitude of forgiveness Christ offered to me, the cost of His death and the sacrifice of His love. Therefore, forgiving all my offenders wasn't even on my radar.

An angry and resentful narrative began to replay in my mind concerning my abortion and my fiancé. A hardening of my heart began to slowly poison my soul. It was so much easier to blame all my problems on Craig and my dad. *They are the ones that caused my pain. They are the reason I am hurting. It's their fault that I feel this way.*

This codependence, attached to all the unhealed trauma and unrepentant sin, was a recipe for disaster. I was living in a downward spiral from abortion, to depression, to PTSD, to suicidal torment, to blaming, anger, and resentment. Down and deep, I kept going. Further from God, further from healing, and further into the mud.

I was like a lamb in the forest, lost, confused, wounded, and running from one muddy pit to another. The wolves continued to chase me down, and my shepherd seemed nowhere to be found.

Off and on for over a year, I began to cheat on my fiancé, who during this time would become my husband. This facade temporarily brought on a delusional sense of "happiness." At times it seemed to numb the pain. It was a perfect trap set by the enemy to deceive me into a warped sense of intimacy and connection which only led me further into bondage. Instead of getting counseling on my own and with my spouse to work through our issues, I chose to selfishly act out. I chose to be in denial. I chose to escape and run. I chose to lie and rationalize that I *deserved* to feel happy.

Doesn't that sound crazy? Cheating on my spouse would make me happy. Where did I even get this idea? It was a twisted and warped perspective, planted into my mind by the enemy. I wish I could go back in time and shake myself awake: *No honey, that's called lust, that's called deception, that's called bondage.*

Instead, I bought the enemy's lies again: *"Cheating is the answer to make you feel better. Come to the mud, friend. The mud is the solution to your problems."*

I justified my husband not giving me the attention that I needed emotionally and relationally as an excuse to commit adultery. My needs were not being met, so I deserved better. I allowed myself to be a pawn to lure yet another person into the enemy's web of destruction for me, for her, and for my husband.

Did you catch that? *Her.*

Yes. The person I cheated on my husband with was a female.

I continued to spiral deeper into the proverbial mud.

When I jumped off that next cliff of spiritual and relational death, the enemy had me convinced this was the path to stop the pain. His solution seemed to work, as there were days I played and lived joyfully in the mud. I lied to myself that the mud was the perfect escape. In the moment, the mud was comforting and pleasant. Sometimes you are so caught up in the mud, you don't even realize *how dirty you have gotten.*

Until the one day that you do.

And then you start seeing the dirt for what it is.

I remember the day when I opened my eyes and realized what I had done, and what I was doing. *"How did I get here? Who is this person? This is not who I am! What is wrong with me? What do I do now? This is a mess. I am a mess. This is so messed up."*

At this point in my story, I was ignorant and blind to the spiritual things taking place in my life. Utterly clueless.

I didn't even know I had an enemy, and I surely didn't think that God cared about anything personal in my life. He was just some force in the sky that was probably waiting to punish me or zap me with a lightning bolt. After all, if God was so good, why did I have the dad I had? Where was God when my mom was pushed down the stairs and bleeding? Where was God during all the abuse? Where was God when that little girl hid under the stairs, and hid under the bed? Where was God when my boyfriend rejected me, rejected our baby? Why didn't God make him change his mind? If He was so loving and powerful, how could God *allow all of that?*

The enemy is so strategic at painting God as the villain. Looking back at my spiritual state back then, it's no wonder I was such an easy prey. In Hosea 4:6 God tells us, "My people perish for lack of knowledge."

My ignorance was my demise. The many lies I believed were destroying me slowly, day by day, one decision at a time.

> "And no wonder, for Satan himself masquerades as an angel of light."
>
> **2 Corinthians 11:14 NIV**

The enemy loved that I didn't know he existed. He wanted me to stay blind. He didn't show up announcing himself with a red suit and a pitchfork. He snuck his way in under a pretense of goodness and truth. He played me and preyed on all of my wounds and weaknesses. He knew exactly how to keep me away from God and how to set up strategic traps and false narratives. His goal was to bring me into sin, suffering, and destruction. He outsmarted me every time. I could not beat him in my self-sufficient human strength or intelligence. I, alone, was no match for the devil.

He wanted to stay hidden from where he was operating in my life. He wanted me to believe, "Jaymee, you aren't too muddy. It's just a little dirt here and there. Your life is not as bad as others. Nothing to alarm you. You are fine, Jaymee. You are totally fine."

I was so blinded and deceived that I even would have told you that I believed in God and that I was a Christian. I would have told you that I was a "good" person compared to most. At least I wasn't out blatantly murdering or kidnapping people, right? Remember, how I served the homeless? Remember, how I went to church a few times? Remember, all the good I had done in my life? I was nice and kind most of the time. I worked hard and loved people. I even had a Bible lying on my coffee table covered in dust. Surely I would make the cut to go to heaven when the time came.

Deceived and covered in dirt. Dripping mud from every crevice of my soul. Completely blind to my wretchedness. Contaminated by sin. Delusional in my measure of "goodness."

So, there I was, perishing like nobody's business. Spiraling, rolling, becoming one with the mud. This time in my life brought on a new level of stress and chaos. I was living a double life, lying to my husband daily. I had emotionally entangled my lover into this mess, and by the time I decided to stop the infidelity, I realized I was fifty feet deep in mud. The harder I tried to retreat and get out, the more the wheels spun and flung mud in every direction. When the enemy has you, he does everything in his power to never let you out. He knows God's love for you, and he knows the best way to take you out: push you deeper in the mud. He discourages, derails, distracts, and tries to lead you into despair. Or worse, he convinces you to cope, manage, and ignore your sin.

Shortly before we got married and for a period of time after, there was a break in the affair. The problem is when you keep things in the dark, it makes it impossible for relationships to heal. We tried counseling, but it remained surface-level in the discussion, and I never revealed my secret. It was like trying to put a Band-Aid on an artery that was bleeding out everywhere.

A few months after our wedding, my older sister attempted to take her life. That event sent me spiraling into the mud again.

> I was an emotional wreck.
> Back into the affair.
> Running.
> Hiding.
> Lying.
> Coping.
> Sinking deeper and deeper.

Eventually, the affair would come to an end, but not without a trail of destruction around me and within me. My husband and I struggled in so many ways in our marriage even after it ended. Our physical intimacy, our communication, our conflict resolution, our financial decisions. Everything was hard. The person who had once been my best friend seemed like a roommate. At times he seemed to be my enemy. I know he was confused most of the time during this season because he didn't understand why things were so broken. At this time, he didn't know there had been an affair. He just saw that he was losing his wife. After the abortion, he had checked out emotionally for a good eight months, but throughout the time of the affair, he sensed something was wrong. He attempted to reconnect and give me more attention, but I was already gone emotionally and mentally.

Craig and I had great chemistry, connection, and interests, but we did not have a healthy understanding of God's definition of marriage. In addition, neither of us had ever had any personal counseling nor did we have wise godly counsel in our lives to help us navigate our immaturity and wounds.

These are just some of the reasons that the divorce rates are so high. Selfishness. No accountability. No relationship with Jesus. No counseling. No unpacking our family of origin dysfunction or past hurts. This is a setup for failure, relationally and spiritually. It was like trying to bake a cake, blindfolded, with all the ingredients but no recipe to follow. Can you imagine what the end product would be? *A hot mess.*

For the next year, Craig and I toiled together doing the best we could with what we had. It seemed that we were heading in the right direction. In May of 2005, my mom said that the only thing she wanted for Mother's Day was for Craig and me to come to church with her. She had been dripping Jesus on us and praying for us for eight years. She never gave up hope and remained faithful in praying for our salvation. She volunteered at church, attended Bible study faithfully, and put our names on every prayer circle list she could find. She had quit smoking, gotten baptized, and invited us to church multiple times. We didn't want to hear anything about faith or church, though. We were good.

Yet, there was a parallel track of good and evil going to war for our souls. The appointed time of God's grace, mercy, love, and forgiveness would penetrate both Craig's and my heart like a two-edged sword. This Mother's Day, we would say yes to the church invitation to Grace Family Church, a non-denominational church in Tampa, Florida. My mother's greatest prayer was for her children to have a divine encounter with the Living God. And on this day, I did.

The saints of heaven were cheering as the Holy Spirit began to drench me in His love. Every word that came out of Pastor Craig Altman's mouth was as if Jesus touched my cheeks ever so softly, looked me directly in the eyes, and said, *"I am real. I am here. I love you. Come to me with all that burdens your soul. I will give you rest. I am here to set you free. Jaymee, will you come to me? Will you trust me?"*

My spirit sensed the words that God had been trying to speak to me for years. *"Do not be afraid Jaymee, for I have redeemed you; I have called you by name. You, Beloved, are mine."*

I sobbed so hard that day. For the first time in my life, I felt a hug from heaven. An embrace from the Creator of the

Universe. His warmth filled my heart in a way I had never felt. Every word was exactly what I needed to hear. He spoke to my deepest pain and my layers of shame. My hardened heart was becoming softened flesh once again. For the next four weeks, Craig and I showed up to church, and the Holy Spirit continued to heal my soul. God's words being shared each week operated in supernatural grace that drew us into His presence like never before. It was full of wisdom and truth, wrapped in His mercy, grace, and forgiveness.

Each week I wept. I couldn't speak. I entered a holy silence. A holy love. A holy transformation within my heart had begun. One by one, the walls I built to protect myself were being torn down into nothing. In just one month of attending church, I was coming to the understanding that not only was God real, He was personal. He cared about me and was speaking directly to me in ways I had never experienced. He loved me. He saw me. He knew me in every way. I still had a ton of questions, but God was meeting me just as I was: a broken, surrendered, muddy mess.

Unbeknownst to us, the real battle was upon us. The great cloud of witnesses and all the angels in heaven were watching the grip of hell loosen on our souls, but hell was not so easily deterred. On June 7th, 2005, our second wedding anniversary, there was an unexpected knock at the door of our apartment as we were preparing to walk out to celebrate with dinner.

Two detectives dressed in blue, badges attached to their hips, were standing with expressions of deep concern. "Are you Jaymee Wallace, ma'am?"

"Yes, I am," I replied.

"May we come inside and ask you a few questions?"

CHAPTER SIX

THE TRUTH WILL SET YOU FREE

"Whoever conceals their sins does not prosper, but the one who confesses and renounces them finds mercy."

Proverbs 28:13 NIV

As Craig and I sat down with the two officers, every ounce of me wanted to crawl in a dark hole or run away. After 30 minutes of asking questions, the two officers left. I knew the moment the door closed behind them that I would have to do one of the hardest things in my life.

I would have to tell my husband the truth.

I had been good at lying, hiding, and denying. I was concealing the truth and running from being honest because I didn't want to face the consequences of my decisions. Sin always comes with a *high price tag*. If I had known what it would cost me when I gave into temptation, I would have run the other way. Oh, how I wish I had run away from the sin that so easily and cunningly entangled me.

Whatever is done in the dark will always be brought to the light. God is just. God hates the darkness and deception, and knows when we are walking in the darkness, it only leads to our destruction. The enemy uses a megaphone of condemnation, shame, and accusation to tell us how bad we are when we fall. God exposes our sins because He loves us, not because he is trying to "catch" us doing the wrong thing and rub it in our faces. God disciplines us because He loves us. He shines His light on our sins because the only way we can heal is in the light.

God knew that if I would get honest about my sin, I could experience true freedom. The weight of secrecy and shame I had been carrying wouldn't be lifted simply because I started going to church and gotten curious about Jesus. I needed it to be exposed to the light of God's truth. God's truth includes getting humble and being real. It means being vulnerable and being honest, with God and, at some point, with others.

The officers left our apartment, and as the echo of the door reverberated through the room, the tears rippled down my cheeks like a torrential rain. My heart was racing 1000 miles per hour. I turned to Craig and began to *confess everything*.

I had cheated on him.

It had been with a female.

And although it was consensual, she had been a high school student who I coached and taught.

Whoa.

I know.

That's a heavy blow.

For most people that I share this with, it feels like they have been sucker punched.

Please stay with me.

I felt so lonely. I felt emotionally rejected by Craig. He was a workaholic and took on so many coaching jobs, so he was rarely home. Of course, none of these things justify my choices. Yet in silent suffering, I began to build a thicker wall of resentment against him. The black hole consumed me. Buried in the pain of killing my unborn child and my husband's absence emotionally and physically, I allowed my personal life to seep into my professional one, into an unlawful sexual relationship with a minor. This went on and off for nearly a year in a half until I finally cut things off because the chaos caught up with me.

> *Even though it was over two decades ago, it's hard for me to even write it. It's hard because it brings to remembrance all the hurt it caused so many people. It's hard because I can't believe I went there and allowed this to happen. It's embarrassing, disgraceful, and something I never thought I could do. How did I get to a place where I would justify an illegal affair with a female student? As regretful as I am, it is also this very disastrous season of my life that ultimately brought me to the foot of the cross. My greatest failure drew me into a personal relationship with the Almighty God.*

Today, I can tell my story with the pain of regret, but *without the weight of shame*. I am not that woman anymore. I have been redeemed, forgiven, transformed, delivered, and set free by the power of Jesus Christ. I am a child of the King of Kings, and He is the only one allowed to define my value. I am not defined by my past now that I am in Christ. I can be labelled, called names, dismissed, persecuted, rejected, and looked down on because of my past, but Jesus has given me a new identity.

Despite that truth, it's incredibly hard to share openly with the world these disgraceful choices that I made. I can understand the shock, disappointment, or even pain that might arise in anyone who hears my story.

Yet where great sin abounds, God's grace abounds even greater. When the darkness is brought into the light, *only then* is all its power stripped away. It takes courage to expose the darkness, to tell the truth about the darkness we have been consumed by and lured into. But it's the truth that sets us free. Nothing is too dark or too wrong to be redeemed by Jesus Christ. His forgiveness and mercy are not for some sins but for *all sins*. At the cross, He paid the debt for it all.

When the police showed up at my door that night, I didn't realize that I was opening the door to a chapter of my life that would result in my healing. My disobedience and dishonesty were weighing heavily on me, even if I did not want to admit it. For the longest time, I had chosen to lie, rationalize, justify, hide, and deny my sin and pain. As a result, I suffered, and I caused others to suffer.

> I lost joy.
> I could not sleep well.
> My body got sick and weakened.
> I felt heaviness.
> I was weary and tired emotionally and mentally.
> I lost my peace and felt anxious.
> I became critical and judgmental of others.
> I couldn't hear God's voice.
> I was distant from God.
> The enemy had access to my mind and heart.
> My closest relationships were stressful.

My mind was tormented with racing thoughts and guilt.

And now, I was face-to-face with this truth that held me captive. I had to confess it to my husband. I knew once I came clean, it was plausible I would lose Craig forever. He had every right to walk away from me and the marriage. Who could blame him?

It was straight-up horrible to admit to the man I loved that I had broken our marriage covenant, brought dishonor to the marriage bed, had lived a lie, and within all that, *committed a crime*. Full of shame, regret, and fear of the future, I awaited his response. With a shocked, distraught, and emotional expression, he hugged me as I wept. Finally, with tears in his eyes, he swallowed hard and said,

"I forgive you, Jaymee. I don't take responsibility for the decisions you made, but I do understand the role I have played. I should have spoken up about the baby; I should have married you instead of allowing fear to control my decisions. I know you are a good woman who was hurting and made some really poor decisions. I will stand by you because you are my wife, and I love you."

I was speechless. Who responds this way? How did I deserve this kind of love? How is any man able to experience this kind of betrayal and still say *I forgive you, I will stand by you, and I love you*? Only a man whose heart had been saturated with the grace of God. Only God could bring this kind of grace, forgiveness, and mercy. Craig chose to be willing to trust God more than his pain. He chose to forgive me, and to love me at my absolute worst.

Grace, upon grace, upon grace.

What is the grace of God? It is the favor of God that no one deserves, and no one could ever earn.

I deserved nothing from Craig. I did not deserve a second chance, but God knew Craig and I could do more for His kingdom together than we could ever accomplish apart. Yes, genuine repentance, surrender, and humbling myself before God and Craig were a requirement. Through this, God could then redeem us, redeem our marriage, and turn everything meant to destroy us into something for our good, to bring hope and healing to other marriages. Our marriage would become an example of God's redemption and healing for other broken marriages.

When a hopeless soul brings their brokenness, sin, failures, and pain to the feet of Jesus, He redeems it all.

Through my confessions, I could now experience:

The joy of the Lord.
The peace of God.
The healing of a loving God.
The forgiveness of God.
The mercy of God.
The grace of God.

God had always been around me, pursuing me, and covering me in His grace even when I didn't know Him. Even though I didn't deserve His grace, He was there in the mud, in the pain, in the valleys, in my rebellion, in my faking, in my hiding. He was always there, waiting for my complete surrender, longing for me to truly know what it felt like to be loved by Him.

His grace triumphed over my sin. His mercy shattered my failure. His love endured my betrayal.

> *" For it is by grace you have been saved, through faith—and this is not from yourselves, it is the gift of God."*
>
> **Ephesians 2:8 NIV**

Neither my husband nor I had fully committed our lives to Jesus at this time, but we felt the presence of God at work in us and all around us. He was speaking to our pain and softening us with His love. As the Holy Spirit was drawing us both into salvation through His grace, He was also working the power of His grace through my husband.

> *"Freely you have received; freely give."*
>
> **Matthew 10:8b NIV**

It doesn't make natural sense that Craig and I have celebrated decades of marriage when you look at what we have been through. But then again, this is the kind of God that we serve. Only He could rewrite our story in a way that shines His love, forgiveness, mercy, and redemption. God is our redeemer. God is in the healing business, and He can take the most horrible sin and pain and transform them into His beauty from the darkest of ashes.

Of course, God's mercy doesn't change the natural consequences for sin in the world we live in. I had broken the law. I had committed a crime. Craig and I were about to be tested even further as I walked out the reality of the devastation my choices caused.

CHAPTER SEVEN

FROM WILDERNESS TO WONDER

"For I am about to do something new. See, I have already begun! Do you not see it? I will make a pathway through the wilderness. I will create rivers in the dry wasteland."

Isaiah 43:19 NLT

I sat in the corner of my closet crying out to God, "Why is this happening?"

The reporters pounded on our apartment door. "We just want to hear your side of the story, Jaymee. Just give us ten minutes."

The media had caught wind that there was an investigation concerning a minor, a teacher, and a sexual relationship. In reality, they didn't want to hear "my side of the story"; they wanted to sensationalize the sin. The media frenzy was so intense that I recall helicopters buzzing around our complex. Reporters called my husband's family in other cities, and my friends and family in other states. It was hard enough to deal with the magnitude of my mess within my close-knit circle, much less have my skeletons on blast publicly across the globe.

And a greater chaos intensified.

I had always struggled with wanting the approval of people. I was a person who wanted to be popular and well-respected. The unfolding of these events eliminated the possibility of any of those comforts. I thought after becoming a Christian my life would be easier, and that God would spare me from any intense suffering. I had owned and taken responsibility for my sin. I had repented, my eyes had been opened, and I had received God's forgiveness, love, and grace! My new life had begun!

But my past was far from behind me. The consequences of my choices would impact me for the next two decades. This time, the only good news was that it was going to be different than the first two decades of my life, because *this time I was walking with Jesus*. Craig and I had given our lives to Jesus in the midst of this chaos, and this decision changed everything.

Jesus changes everything for the better. But better does not mean easier.

Better does not mean comfortable. Walking with Jesus doesn't mean all sunshine and rainbows. As I dove deeper into the gospels, I quickly found that suffering, self-denial, and sacrifice were part of the journey of following Jesus. As a new Christian, I didn't understand how to calculate the cost to follow him, nor the dying of self it would require. All I knew was that *He was all I had*, and that my faith in Christ was the only way through this mess.

I don't blame God for any of the suffering I endured. I made the choices which led to the suffering.

God didn't cause the affliction, *but He allowed it.*

To strengthen my faith.

To draw me into a deeper intimacy with Him.

To remove the dross around my heart.

To transform my character into the likeness of His Son.

And so, the work in my soul had begun. Suffering beyond what I could have ever imagined rolled in like an afternoon thunderstorm. Crashing. Booming. Pouring. Intensifying from a Category Two Hurricane to a Cat Five without warning.

God, where the heck are you?

Within a few months of becoming a new Christian, I would be arrested, lose my job, lose our apartment, and lose a baby. Friends and family would abandon us, condemn us, and reject us. All hell had broken loose. Everything was falling apart.

The media frenzy with helicopters, video cameras, phone harassment, propaganda, truth, lies, and my sin blasted on the internet from here to Japan, along with any version of the story that would sell. Oprah called. Greta Jones called. Dozens more reporters pounded on my door to glorify the sin story and get the juicy gossip. My mug shot was in the newspaper, and radio talk shows turned my life disaster into their comic relief. It was pure hell.

I was working in an office downtown with a pending investigation into my case. Everyone I worked with knew why I was there. I was given the job to stuff envelopes for eight hours a day, five days a week. This was very humbling, considering I had a degree in mathematics and had taught in the classroom for seven years before working in the corporate world. Yet this job gave me daily divine appointments with my Savior. I stuffed those envelopes as unto the Lord, and knowing the truth of my situation, I was grateful for a paycheck. My heart and eyes were freshly awakened to the gospel. I devoured my Bible during every break and ate by myself at lunch so I could hear the whispers of Jesus through His word.

Jesus spoke to my scared heart every day. His Word came alive and jumped off the pages as if He were sitting with me in that office. I couldn't believe how real, personal, and loving God was. When our hearts are humbled and open to receive, that's when we see the face of God. I felt refreshment, joy, and fulfillment in every crevice of my soul. I no longer felt empty, and all I wanted was Him. His voice and His truth drowned out all the noise that was trying to consume my attention. I was so afraid of what my future held, but simultaneously, I felt at peace because of *Him*.

As the waves were crashing around me, His voice brought a consistent beckoning to trust Him when nothing seemed to be going right. This was faith: trusting when I couldn't see, believing that God would use even this mess for good.

I'll never forget the day when they decided to make an arrest. It was October 31st, 2005, just three months after giving my life to Jesus and two weeks after being baptized with my husband. The arresting officer was kind and allowed me to call my husband as he drove me to Orient Jail in Tampa. Panic started to creep in. A tightening in the chest. Rapid breathing. Clammy, cold hands. Racing thoughts. Racing heartbeats. I was in disbelief that this was my life. Was this *actually happening*?

As we pulled up to the jail, he said, "Jaymee, I have to put these handcuffs on now."

I went into booking, and I felt nothing but terror. I had never committed a crime, been arrested, or broken the law beyond a speeding ticket. Jail felt like a nightmare coming true. For five hours, I sat sobbing in disbelief and regret. I felt eyes from all directions fixated on me. My head hung with shame and despair. With one shallow breath, I finally prayed, *"I need you, God, please help me, Jesus."*

An immediate rest came over my trembling body like a cloud of light and peace. Jesus whispered back, *"You are mine. I'm not letting you go. Everything will be ok. Hold onto me, Jaymee, I'm not done with you yet."*

God wants to whisper His truth and love to us in the chaos of the fire. It's in the moments of our stillness, desperation, and surrender that He will speak peace. His presence changes everything. Of course, God had always been there, but it was astonishing how much my senses felt His presence in a time like this.

Right after Craig and I gave our lives to the Lord, the scales began to fall from our eyes. We had a hunger and thirst to know Jesus more, and we were at church more than anywhere else. We began attending Bible studies together and joined our first small group with other young married couples at church. I started counseling with my spiritual mama, Marilyn, and walked through post-abortion healing with my counselor, Kelli. Craig started meeting with Pastor Doug, and God began to do a mighty work in us individually and in our marriage. Our hearts were singing, celebrating, and praising God for this new internal freedom.

I remember reading the story in Exodus about the journey of the Israelites. God delivered His people from slavery in Egypt and then took them into the desert. A *wilderness.*

In that season, we knew that God had delivered us from "Egypt" and the kingdom of darkness, and we had so much hope for this new life we were walking in together. God was redeeming our story and our relationship day by day. New mercies poured onto us each morning. Even though God had not resolved our legal circumstances, He had given us new joy, new peace, and a new trust that He was good and that He would take care of us no matter what.

But before the flourishing, we would travel through the wilderness.

Scorched land.

Parched mouths.

Vast desert.

Scarce food.

The wilderness was lonely, and it was uncomfortable. God stripped us of everything except for Him, not to abandon us, but to be alone with us. He wanted our undivided attention in the desert. Our destiny and greatest assignments for the kingdom are birthed in the wilderness seasons of our lives. The hotter the fire in the desert, the greater impact our healing and restoration will have in the world.

God wanted to use the desert to grow us. To refine us. To prepare us.

Satan wanted to use the desert to destroy us. To turn us back to sin. To get us to complain and wallow in self-pity and despair.

I must be honest. In the jail on that day of my arrest, I was falling into despair as the walls of my freedom closed in on me. I was just a baby Christian, and I wasn't convinced I could handle this kind of wilderness.

I had to choose how to respond to this season of my life.

This was a key moment in my walk with Christ. The storm raged around me in chaos with sand, dirt, and tumbleweed blowing from every direction. All comfort was removed. Nothing I saw in the natural circumstances reflected the promises of God we had been praying over our lives. Would I allow the suffering to cause me to give up? Would I abandon my faith? Would our marriage withstand this new fire? Would we "run back to Egypt" and our old, sinful habits?

The enemy will tempt us with pleasure to help take away the desert's discomfort, or he will pounce on our pain to get us to turn from God and crumble. He comes after baby Christians because he's so angry he lost another soul from hell, so he sets out to weaken our witness. He sets out to destroy our testimony and make our faith look like a fraud. He tries to lure us into bondage and sin.

Yet, God's plan is always to use the wilderness for our good.

The heat of the desert either destroys or refines.

My husband bailed me out of jail. We didn't know what the future would hold, but we knew God's truth, we loved Jesus, we loved our church family, and we loved each other. We knew that the awesome Creator of the earth was alive in us and with us through this inferno. We decided to cling tighter to Jesus through the fire. When all seemed out of control, we could rest on the one who was in control.

We had a community of strong Christians from our church that stood beside us. The fiery darts of persecution were being aimed at us *and* at them. They loved us, prayed with us, and walked out their faith when it was not popular, comfortable, or easy. God protected and sustained us through that time through His Church and His people.

Instead of throwing stones, they washed our feet.

Instead of walking in self-righteousness, they invited us in and bandaged our wounds.

Instead of fleeing the heat of the fire, they stood in the fire *with us*.

They encouraged us and spoke God's hope into our situation. They spoke truth and love. They embraced us in the darkest time of our lives. I didn't deserve their mercy, forgiveness, or grace, but that's the kind of love God calls the church to.

How did they do this?

They laid hands on us and prayed over us and with us.

They invited us into their homes and broke bread with us.

They helped us sell furniture so we could pay our legal fees.

They loved us when it wasn't popular to do so.

They mentored us and invited us to Bible Study.

They grieved with us at the loss of our child.

Yes. We lost the baby. Two days after Craig bailed me out of jail, we found out I was pregnant. What a mix of emotions! I had always wanted to be a mom, but this was a crazy time to contemplate the idea of motherhood. Nevertheless, we trusted God with our story and believed he could redeem the pain of the loss of our first child. Then, three months into the pregnancy, our little one went to heaven. We were devastated. We were heartbroken. And yet we were held in the love and prayers of our church community who would not abandon us to suffer on our own.

One man, Joe, led the class for new believers at our church. The first night there were 20 people, but for the next six months it was just me and Craig who showed up. Every Wednesday night, Joe was faithful to pour into us. He loved us and answered our questions. Many times I would just weep, especially when he taught on God's grace. The Lord knew Craig and I needed that undivided attention. So many times in church we measure success with numbers and big classes. I will testify that Joe's faithfulness to teach for "just two people" was foundational to Craig and me in our early years of following Christ.

The church *showed up*. They lived out what they said they believed. They chose to trust more in God's plan of redemption than in a worldly justice system of punishment and retribution. They followed the example of Christ in demonstrating a sacrificial, costly, embodied love. They taught us about the truth that Jesus' death on the cross paid the price for our sins, and they looked upon me with the same mercy, grace, and forgiveness that they were teaching me about. I witnessed the truth of God's love, not just in theory, but in practice.

As Craig and I were prayerfully navigating the long and drawn-out process of criminal proceedings, we unexpectedly conceived our son Tyson Isaiah. We met this news both with joy and fear as we did not know what the future would hold. The time for trial was drawing near. What if I went to prison? What would this do to our family? God doesn't make mistakes, but this increased the stakes. Children are always a blessing from the Lord, but how could this be the right time? I couldn't wait to be a mom and expand our family, but the stress of the impending sentencing was a lingering cloud of doom.

Internally, I was struggling because I wanted to take responsibility for my actions, but some of the accusations were not accurate. On paper, I could face ten to thirty years in prison. The idea of that potential outcome still puts a rock into the pit of my stomach. I remember the nausea, the strain, the fear of what was to come. The weight on my heart as a mama was indescribable.

Sin will always cost you more than you anticipated.

I spent night after night with my husband, praying, laying hands on my head, begging God to just help me fall asleep. I felt crippled by fear as the tears streamed down my face, night after night. This was a worst-case scenario. Here I was, on fire for Jesus, healing taking place in my marriage, pregnant, and this unimaginable possibility of heavy prison time pressing down on me daily. The desert seemed to stretch endlessly before me as the timetable for the legal proceedings continued to be delayed. Coincidentally, the prosecutor of my case was also pregnant, which pushed the court dates further out. She wanted to keep the case, so it was postponed.

The time came for me to give birth to our beautiful baby boy, Tyson. After forty hours of labor, I was rushed into an emergency c-section to save my life and the life of my baby. Due to the difficult recovery I was facing, the legal timetable was pushed back again. God's ways are higher. God's timing is always perfect. Somehow, we were given those first few months with our son as we waited for the trial.

Tyson's birth brought on greater joy, hope, and intimacy within our expanded family. God was restoring, healing, and showing His love and provision in every way. His hand was surely on us, and Craig and I grew closer to each other and to Jesus as we dedicated our son to the Lord.

When Tyson was just a few months old, we needed to decide to take a deal, go to trial, or plead guilty with an open plea to the judge. I can't begin to express how much was at stake with this decision. We prayed and fasted and sought the Lord's will with all our hearts and souls. God gives wisdom generously to those who ask. He had been faithful through the fire and was not about to abandon us now.

After days and days of prayer, I chose to do an open plea of guilty to the court. I had no previous criminal background, and since so many people were willing to testify to my character in court, this seemed like the best thing to do. Our legal team thought I would be able to take responsibility for my actions, and at most be sentenced to house arrest so I could keep my new little family intact.

On December 5th, 2007, God would have a different plan.

"Jaymee Wallace, you are sentenced to three years in prison."

I couldn't comprehend the words that rolled off the judge's lips. The courtroom full of people gasped in disbelief, my mom passed out, and my husband wept as he fell to his knees. My chest caved in pain and breathlessness as my heart shattered into a million pieces. They put me in handcuffs and didn't let me say goodbye. Just a few feet outside the courtroom, my cousin, Joy, held my ten-month-old son. He was reaching for his mama, but his little hands would not get to touch mine again for many weeks.

Wrecked is an understatement. Tears fall down my face and my body trembles to this day every time I relive those memories. Surely, because I had repented and began to serve and follow Jesus, God would spare me of this kind of suffering?

Surely *prison* would not be my wilderness.

God had just healed our marriage. We had overcome an insurmountable betrayal, and now we faced three years of separation? God has just given us a son, after the devastating losses we had experienced. And now our family would be torn apart?

"God, what are you doing? Why God, why? God, why have you forsaken me?"

Due to my emotional state, I would be put into solitary confinement for ten days. In these early days of being in the "desert", God would bring me to solitude, so my attention was all His. I was spiraling into confusion, anger, disbelief, panic, and despair. This was my ultimate nightmare coming true.

I was just wandering in the desert with no hope of seeing my promised land.

Shackled.
Barefoot.
Cold.
Alone.
Distressed.

Clothed in an orange jumpsuit, I would spend 23 hours a day with God and my Bible in a small, cold, cement cell. In the silence and devastation, I had nothing to cling to except

His presence. I needed Him to help me understand His plan for my life. I needed fresh provision of hope and strength.

Face down on a cement floor of a box the size of a bathroom, I wept and waited. *Jesus laid down next to me.* With my head buried in my tear-soaked arms, He told me to lift my head up.

He spoke to my heart, *"And when you are perfected in Me, Jaymee, you shall be released to bring blessing back to the sea of humanity from whence you came."*

In that cell, I remembered the stories of Paul and Joseph, heroes of the faith who were imprisoned for seasons of their lives. One day a prisoner, the next a mighty vessel to be used for God's glory. God needed to set me apart even from my *good* distractions to prepare me in the wilderness for greater assignments. God imparted His word deep into my heart as I lay down on that cold, cell floor in a puddle of agony.

I surrendered once again.

It's amazing to me that within hours they were ready to medicate me into some numb, zombie-like emotional state, but it would take three days to get a Bible. You never realize how much you thirst for God's word until you don't have the freedom to read it.

I refused the medication and waited for Jesus' bread of life.

Hope would arise once again.

I read the Holy Scriptures like they were my only lifeline, my anchor in the storm, my water in the desert. Hebrews 5:8 NIV, "He learned obedience from what he suffered." Isaiah

48:10 NIV, "I have tested you in the furnace of affliction." Romans 5:3 NIV, "Suffering produces perseverance." Genesis 50:20 NLT, "You intended to harm me, but God intended it all for good." I soaked up His Word like a sponge, drawing His living water to coexist with the deep wells of my suffering.

It was in the wilderness and captivity where I would rely on no one but God. I would be tested, purified, and brought forth as gold. I couldn't see it at the time, but my temporary suffering was nothing compared to his "glory to be revealed" (Romans 8:18 NIV).

In that cell the size of a small bathroom, in handcuffs, fed through a slot, I wept. With breast milk still leaking from my breasts, I prayed. I read the Word night and day. I agonized in the pain of losing my worldly freedoms and being ripped from my family.

I would feel the crushing sensation each time I saw my red, swollen-eyed husband and my ten-month-old infant son kissing the window, crying out for his mommy during visitation. Separated from me by a clear, plastic wall, Tyson would pound his little fists in protest. He was so confused as to why he couldn't touch his mama and hold his mama. Part of my soul felt like it died each time as the breast milk would release. We both longed to snuggle as mother and child should.

My little family cared for me faithfully every single day, with letters, phone calls, visits, and unwavering support. I marveled at this man God gave to me as a husband. He chose to step up in every way as a father and as a spouse when it would have been so much easier just to abandon me. Craig and I had not been apart more than seven days in ten years.

Every day my family left from my one-hour visit to Orient Road jail, I would weep on my knees crying to God like Jesus, "If there is another way…"

The Holy Spirit comforted me.

Jaymee, I formed you in the womb, I knew you before you were born, you will be my messenger of hope. There will be power in your testimony to preach the good news of my grace being fully sufficient. I am with you. I am leading you, and I will rescue you at the right time. Will you trust me? Continue to put my Word in your heart and I will provide everything you need.

I will restore.
I will heal your land.
I will pay back double what the locusts have stolen.
My inheritance is your portion.
My word does not return void.
But first, I need you to abide in me.

Trust me with your son, for he is my child first. Trust me with your marriage, for it is your most important human relationship. Trust me with your time in the desert, for I am going to use your foolish things to confound the wise of the world for my glory. You will tell the story of my faithfulness and love. You will tell the story of how you lost your earthy freedom, and that story will set others free.

> "The more I have the courage to meet God in this place of weakness, the more I will know myself to be truly and deeply loved by God. And the more deeply I know this love, the easier it will be to trust it as Christ did - preferring God's will to my own."[3]
> **C.S. Lewis**

---

[3] Mead, M. L. (2020, May 20). *In times of uncertainty: Encouragement from C. S. Lewis.* Wheaton College.
https://www.wheaton.edu/news/recent-news/2020/may/in-times-of-uncertainty/

CHAPTER EIGHT

PRISON PRESSURE

"Let the redeemed of the LORD tell their story— those he redeemed from the hand of the foe."

Psalm 107:2 NIV

In the middle of the night, an officer at Orient Road jail woke me with the news, "Wallace, get up, you are being transferred to prison tonight."

With my hands and feet shackled, I shuffled outside in my orange jumpsuit, shivering and half asleep. It was a brisk 40 degrees as I boarded a long, white bus with all the windows covered. The floor was wet and cold. It smelled musty, and I felt like I was getting into a moving dungeon.

Women from other jails were also being transferred that night, and the bus was filled with a thick cloud of grief and despair. Fear raced up and down my spine as I looked into their hardened, unfriendly faces. I shuddered as I sat down and tried to gaze out the window with a thin strip of light trying to break through. I fixated on that light of hope, so I didn't have to embrace the darkness around me.

Upon our arrival at the prison, we were screamed at and ushered into a room like cattle. We would have to strip completely down to nothing to ensure we weren't trying to bring contraband into the prison.

> Naked.
> Afraid.
> Humiliated.

I was surrounded by twenty other women but felt desperately alone.

The enemy attempted to strip us of all dignity. Tears streaming down my face, all I could pray was the name of Jesus as my chest shook with every breath. This feeling would intensify as we were sprayed with ice-cold water and an awful-smelling shampoo to ensure we didn't have lice. As I walked through the gates, large towers loomed in the sky with men holding AK-47 guns.

This was Lowell Correctional Institution in Ocala, FL. At that time, it was the largest women's prison in the United States.

> *Is this a horror movie?*
> *Is this my life?*
> *Lord, how is this the plan?*

There was a stench of cigarette smoke that floated across the room, making it difficult to breathe. Because I had asthma and was very allergic to smoke, my eyes and nose burned, and I couldn't imagine trying to sleep in my new "home." The officers seemed like Satan's assigned tormentors. They verbally harassed us in every communication, addressing us only by our inmate number, dehumanizing us to the point of despair. Every move we made felt like walking on thin ice.

To them, we weren't worth much of anything.
We were undignified criminals.
We deserved what we got.

It was just me, Jesus, prayer, and the word of God.
If you want to know how to survive the desert, that's it.
Welcome to prison.
Welcome to God's plan for this redemption story.

> *"O Lord, hear me as I pray; pay attention to my groaning. Listen to my cry for help, my King and my God, for I pray to no one but you."*
>
> **Psalm 5:1-2 NLT**

I could write another book on the things that I endured while incarcerated. Daily, ambulances would roar and wail by our warehouse of 90 bunk beds, racing their way to try and save the women in solitary confinement who tried to take their own lives. The deceptive spirit of death was seeking to destroy more souls, luring them out of emotional pain. Many of them were lifers or had 20-year sentences.

The rapes and the rumors of rapes led me to desperately plead the blood of Jesus over myself and pray for a hedge of protection around my mind and my body. Psalm 91 would be my lifeline. Many days, I didn't think I would make it, but what about the women without Jesus? How did they endure? I could not imagine.

After six weeks of only being able to contact my family through letters, I would be transferred further away to a prison in the panhandle of Florida. My family would visit me every other weekend, and we would talk on the phone, trying to maintain a nurtured relationship. Their world was turned completely upside down in adjusting to my absence.

And yet, God's people rallied. My mom and my husband balanced raising Tyson and working their jobs. Our best friends from church, Dwane and Indera, helped care for Tyson when Craig needed it. My spiritual mama, Marilyn, wrote to me every week. My Bible study girls came from four hours away to visit me. Friends and family sent letters and books to help sustain me. I praise God for such an awesome support system of friends, church family, and loved ones. Despite the pain I caused, many stood by me, and I am forever grateful. That is Jesus. That is the Body of Christ. That is forgiveness. That is the mercy of God. I didn't deserve their love, compassion, and grace upon grace upon grace.

But they loved me anyway.

Jehovah Jireh.
God provides all that we need.
Daily manna in the desert.

I did an eight-month resident Bible Study and Life Principles program where I was worshiping, praying, and reading the Word eight hours a day. Financial freedom, anger resolution, God's design for children and marriage, spiritual warfare, praying and fasting, roots of rejection and healing, forgiveness, and many other life topics were taught straight from the Word of God. I had never felt the anointing or the power of God in my life as I did then. The healing He did in my heart overwhelms me with gratitude.

All this *while in prison*.
God was strengthening me.
Jesus soothed me in my grief.

His Word sustained me.
He was all I had.

I would sit on my bunk and feel the constant presence of the Holy Spirit like never before. He would have me praying with people and sending scriptures to people around me, even some officers at times. Most of the inmates were walking time bombs of pain, anger, despair, and fear. We had no A/C, no heat, and food that was hardly edible. We all desperately needed His hope, as we had been stripped of every comfort we had ever known.

Yet, during this time, I would hear the voice of God and feel His presence stronger than any other time in my life. The intimacy I had with Him is indescribable. I like to imagine it similar to how God used to walk through the Garden of Eden with Adam and Eve. He was so personable to me and so close. Jaymee and Jesus were in constant tension with the pressures in prison, in a heavenly rhythm, walking hand in hand.

Expectantly, the spiritual warfare I witnessed was intense. Everyone was captive within the walls of this prison, and the heavenly armies went to battle for souls. It was surreal. So many women were broken and in need of the love and hope of Jesus Christ. Jesus pursued them to set them free, while the enemy fought to keep them bound and lead them to further destruction.

In a place like prison, the reality of spiritual warfare was very much visible.

On one occasion, a fight broke out between two women. Screaming, cursing, angry, and in pain, they attacked each other, not realizing who the real enemy was. Like fallen dominos, two more women started fighting just three bunks over. Another five bunks over, another pair started going at it. It was unreal. The sense of anger, rage, hatred, strife, and violence consumed our "home."

Not too long after that, I was transferred into a dorm where inmates would live until we were assigned a job. When I arrived at the new dorm, I had a 102 degree fever and a bad case of the flu. I was sick as a dog. I was also new "bait," fresh off the bus. An inmate approached me, demanding I give her some of my "canteen", which is what they called the food and hygiene items you can purchase while in prison when your family puts money on your books. I could tell she was the one who ran the dorm, not the officers. When I politely told her, "No," she began going off on me loudly, calling me every name in the book, along with some choice racial slurs. I crawled into my bunk, desperately wanting to sleep, and began praying.

Gossip travels fast in prison.

By count time that night, she had somehow learned of my charges. As the officer in charge of count exited our dorm into his officer bubble, that same inmate started announcing my charges across the dorm as loud and proud as she could. I was mortified to say the least. I hadn't been in prison 24 hours, and the enemy was already accusing, lying, attacking, and trying to get me thinking he was in charge there. What he didn't calculate is that those labels were not my identity, and it was that tainted past that would take him down through my testimony. I wasn't going to give her the pleasure of answering to those names. I was a daughter of the king, and that was that.

There was an uncomfortable tension in the room after this inmate made her public service announcement at my expense. Was I embarrassed? Absolutely. But the Spirit of God nudged me and reminded me, *"Pray for your enemies and those who persecute you. Remember Jaymee, I am your defender."*

I prayed and rested in His stillness. I forgave her and I went to sleep.

The next morning, there was a shift change. The new officer that was on duty was a hot mess herself. Obnoxious. Mean. Loud. She cursed and yelled at us regularly. She looked the part in her freshly pressed white officer uniform, but you best believe she could easily be wearing blue scrubs.

Well, the "boss" of the dorm, who had previously made her public announcement, woke up even more angry and agitated than before. The officer made a comment about her living area not being up to par, and that was all it took. The inmate barked back at her, and the next thing I know, she's being cuffed and headed to confinement, cursing up a storm. She had lived in this same dorm for the last ten years, but on this day, one day after my arrival, the Lord saw fit to move her elsewhere.

"I am your defender, Jaymee."

It was spiritual warfare right before my eyes. God's divine protection surrounded me in this place of darkness and pain. But it wasn't all dark. In fact, some of the most brilliant light I have experienced came during my prison days. Can I just testify about the worship and intercessory prayer in prison?

If you have never volunteered for prison ministry, I highly recommend it. It most certainly will change your life even more than the inmates you seek to serve. There we were, in a small chapel filled with ladies in blue, fully surrendered and face down on the floor, singing, praising, and crying out to God.

Hearts raw in submission.
Lamenting.
Longing for His presence.

There is never a time that the Spirit of God is closer than during a time of lamenting worship. Oh, what a symphony of the Spirit poured out on His precious daughters in blue. He heard the humility, earnestness, and surrender in our cries. His love was a warm blanket, nestling around our hearts. I've never witnessed any prayer or worship session close to what I experienced with my ladies in that prison chapel.

Dreams, visions, and divine revelations flowed just like breathing. Despite all that I endured while being in prison, heaven opened daily. In the desert, I encountered the Living God, unlike any other time in my life.

Yet, there was intense, continual opposition. I caught head lice twice. I caught MRSA staph (an antibiotic resistant, flesh-eating bacteria), which was *killing* women. I had to live in a cesspool of human waste for two weeks due to broken plumbing. It was miserable, but I was learning to be content without comfort and cleanliness.

The prayers of those in my life encamped God's angels around me. His protection would repel the enemy from consuming me. Even when it *seemed* like the enemy was winning, I knew I had the victory because of the scriptures that were prayed over me. I reminded myself daily to stand firm, and to trust that my story would be used for His glory.

Then there was the struggle of being a mama in prison. I was so afraid of Tyson not knowing me. I was on my knees daily, praying for that child and writing to him in my journal. God said, *"Jaymee, Tyson is my child first. You will have to do all your mothering on your knees in prayer, but trust me, you will see the fruit."*

And hallelujah, did I see the fruit. After days and nights of crying out to God for Tyson for two and a half years, he became a prayer warrior at age five. With child-like faith, my little evangelist started sharing the gospel everywhere he went. His faith was pure. He would throw his hands in the air, worship and sing praises to God, dance with all his heart, and memorize scripture.

One journal entry from prison when Tyson was just one year old on May 7th, 2008, read:

My sweet child Ty! Hi pumpkin! The Lord revealed a vision of the calling on your life, son. I envisioned you on a stage, wearing jeans and a t-shirt, a handsome young man. You were preaching the gospel! To hundreds! Praise God! Tyson, you are called and chosen, my son. Oh, how I pray that you choose to invite Christ into your life and make Him Lord of your life! I'm praising God now because I know He will woo you and draw you near. Son, God has so much in store for you! He promises to make your paths straight and bring His blessing over your life when you choose to follow Him and be all in. God is faithful, son. He loves you just the way you are, but He will mature you and purify you through trials and tribulations and times of suffering to have you become more like Jesus! God will use these times for preparation of divine assignments in your life. You are the head, not the tail, you are blessed in your coming and going!

All my children will be taught by the Lord and great will be their peace! Hallelujah! I love you, Tyson!

Xoxo
Love, Mama

Just six years later, Tyson would be at a Summer Vacation Bible School at a local church. He got invited up on stage to do a Bible trivia competition. When I picked him up that day, he said, "Mama! I got to answer a whole bunch of questions on stage today. Mama, do you think one day I could be on stage and tell hundreds of people about Jesus and share the good news just like Joyce Meyer does?"

My eyes swelled with tears of joy. God was planting seeds in Tyson's heart on His calling that matched the vision I had gotten and prayed over while I was journaling in prison. Oh, the power of a mama's prayer. Never underestimate praying for your children, no matter how old they are.

During my incarceration, the closer I felt to God, the more attacks there were on my marriage and my family. I praise God that my husband was able to remain faithful to our marriage for almost three years physically, but the enemy tried to wear him down mentally. I know it was not an easy battle for him. The last 15 months of my sentence, our marriage almost didn't make it. We were both growing weary. Tyson was starting to be impacted each time they left. It was too much.

I thought God would bring me home early.
But He didn't.

Craig and I both struggled trying to nurture a relationship that pretty much only involved letter writing and holding hands with a kiss hello and a kiss goodbye once or twice a month. I gained a new understanding of why 80% of marriages where a spouse is incarcerated end in divorce. Thank God we had built such a strong foundation before we were separated for two and a half years, but I'm not going to lie and say that we didn't consider ending our marriage throughout my absence and initial return. As hard as it was on my mama's heart to be away, I'm so grateful for Tyson during those years. God gave us this precious reminder of our marriage covenant, and our love for him served as a glue to keep our family together.

After I finished the faith-based program, I moved into a "regular" dorm and got a job at the recreation department teaching fitness classes. A new officer had just started down there, and the evil in her eyes would penetrate your soul and make the hair on your neck stand. She harassed me, *constantly*. At first, I couldn't figure it out, but then I realized that there was something about my love and encouragement that she couldn't stomach. I had started a sticky note ministry, passing out God's word to encourage women at work. It made her angry.

One day, this officer shouted at me, "*Wallace, what are you doing?*"

She snatched the sticky note as I gently answered, "Encouraging people, ma'am."

Well, ten days later, she put me in solitary confinement. I had to wait there, pending investigation, although there was nothing to investigate. She was not too fond of white people, especially not ones who were in a biracial marriage.

There was a lot of racial tension at this facility between the staff. The racial ignorance from all sides at this institution was so heartbreaking, even within the faith community. The strife and division poisoned so many people and programs there. I'm grateful for the men and women who volunteered from outside of the prison, because they stirred my faith and helped me love Jesus even more. They were truly the hands and feet of Jesus, and they loved us all the same. They didn't see women in blue scrubs. They didn't see our charges and scarlet letters. They saw us as daughters of the king. But this officer saw things very differently.

So, there I sat in solitary confinement in the middle of the winter.

This time, I was imprisoned innocently.

I could hardly believe I had been persecuted for my sticky note ministry.

It was so cold in that cell I had to put socks over my hands and put all my clothes on just to stay warm. They fed me through a slot, and the lights stayed on day and night. In confinement, you slept on a big cement slab with a blanket and pillow. But this wasn't my first time in solitude, and I knew how to rely on Jesus.

Our faithful Father brought His *rhema* within His word. Jesus and I had the sweetest, most intimate fellowship. His presence and His word would be my daily bread. I never thought I could pray and read my Bible as long as I did. It was just me and Jesus, day and night, while I would listen to the screams of women who couldn't handle the isolation echoing through our cells.

Lord, when will I be released? How long do I have to endure this? How long Lord, how long?

Little did I know they could hold you in confinement for up to six months "pending an investigation." My unjust imprisonment was right before Thanksgiving, and my family was coming to visit me. My husband called the prison incessantly, but they offered no answers. I only got to see the outside twice in ten days. I showered only twice in a box the size of a small phone booth.

After about eight days with no answer or resolution for my investigation, I was starting to get restless. On the ninth day, I was in my cell crying out to the Lord, on my knees praying for my rescue, when anxiety and claustrophobia started to creep in. I was reading in one of my devotionals, and this was the scripture for that day:

> *"Do not be afraid of what you are about to suffer. I tell you, the devil will put some of you in prison to test you, and you will suffer persecution for ten days. Be faithful, even to the point of death, and I will give you life as your victor's crown."*
>
> **Revelation 2:10 NIV**

As I finished reading this scripture, my heart was overwhelmed with God's peace. No one will ever convince me that God doesn't speak to His people! I *knew* I was about to be released. Oh, how God is so faithful!

The next morning, on the tenth day, I was released from confinement. My God is my Deliverer! The enemy was trying to silence me from spreading the gospel and God's hope at my workplace, but God used it for my good. I had ten days of quiet solitude with my precious Savior. That solitude was a *gift*.

On June 21st, 2010, two and a half years after my conviction, I was released from prison. This release came after serving my full sentence, which was a three-year term with a possible 180 days of "gain time" for good behavior. When I first arrived to prison, I met with my classification officer and told her I planned on not losing a single day of gain time so I could be reunited with my family at two and a half years instead of three. She laughed, mocked me, and insulted me, knowing that officers can take time away for negligible offenses, like having a wrinkled bed, or looking at an officer wrong. Well, God's favor and protection brought my goal to life. I didn't lose a single day of gain time, and at two and a half years, I was released to go home.

But the wilderness season of trial wasn't over.

Our marriage was really on eggshells because I had emotionally withdrawn. It's difficult to explain how much you have to adjust your approach to life when incarcerated. It truly was like being on a different planet. I was grateful to meet a group of women in prison, and we had each other's backs. There's a bond that takes place when you are in survival mode together. I kept in touch with some of them upon my release, but life happens, and people move in different directions. I'm sure we could meet each other on the street today and hug like it was yesterday, when we were stuck inside the barbed wire fence together. But outside of those bonds, intimacy with people on the outside felt so much harder after the isolation of prison.

The separation had worn me and Craig down. I was distant and trying to create a "normal" life again. Craig was angry and frustrated, expecting me to be the same person I was when I left.

I wasn't.

Prison changes you.

I still had my faith, and I was grateful to be home with my family.

But I couldn't change the reality of my experience, and I couldn't rush a return to normalcy.

Shortly after my arrest, we moved in with my mom. Craig and Tyson remained there during my incarceration so she could help Craig with taking care of Tyson. There was an immense amount of tension in my mom's house because my forty-year-old sister had come to live with them. After almost dying from alcoholism, my sister was also suffering from bipolar disorder and schizophrenia, and it was a dark time. My mom had been through some harrowing years. She lost me to prison, her dad died, and then she almost lost her oldest daughter. This stress created serious heart health problems for her.

Besides my initial incarceration, the first three months I was home were some of the hardest times of my life. There we were, trying to put our life back together in the midst of extreme hardship and turmoil. Craig was maxed out, I was at my threshold, and right before our breaking point, I was released. I had to learn to be a mom all over again. I had to participate in mending my marriage all over again. And we found ourselves in a very unstable home environment all over again, due to my sister's mental health struggles.

All hell broke loose because the terms under which I was expecting to serve probation were not what I anticipated. It was a total nightmare because of the nature of my charges. I had to deal with probation conditions which made being a stay-at-home mom almost impossible due to the financial strain and all the restrictions. I was trapped in my mom's house, with my mentally and physically ill sister. Although I was elated to be "free," I still felt like I was in prison.

Craig and I were planning on getting a place of our own as soon as I was released, but there were challenging probation restrictions on where I could live. My mom's place was the only one of our options that was approved. During my initial sentencing, the judge didn't deem it necessary for me to have to be a registered sex offender nor do sex offender probation, yet the way the law is written he didn't have jurisdiction to override the law. The victim testified in court that our encounter was consensual, however, the law stated that I must carry the title of sex offender. I was thrown into the same bucket as anyone who has molested a child or raped someone. These conditions brought on many new challenges in my life as a mother.

My probation ended 18 months early with great favor from God and the judge in February 2012. By the grace of God, I was released from *all* restrictions concerning children, but the scarlet letter remains. I have been transformed by the blood of the Lamb of God and am a new creation in Christ. Yet, even though I took responsibility for my sin, repented, and spent decades in counseling and church, this label remains, based on my past. This has been a very difficult "life sentence" for our family.

The transition period from prison to "freedom" was stressful and hard.

No one can prepare you for it.

At times it felt harder than being in prison.

Craig and I were arguing constantly, and I was forced to attend therapy meetings with 15 other men and listen to their stories. I was one of only two women in this group, and I would leave sobbing because I couldn't listen to certain things so graphic in nature. Men and women are very different, and this mandatory group therapy was devastating to my mental health.

Craig and I would pray over my mind, body, and soul each week, pleading the blood of Jesus.

God poured out His grace over us again.

I was finally permitted to do one on one therapy with a counselor instead of group therapy. Once again, our church family stepped in. Pastor Doug and Mama Marilyn did some marriage counseling with us. I went through the post-abortion healing program called *Surrendering the Secret* at church. I met some of my best friends to this day through our MOPS mom's group at church. God began to rebuild our lives outside of the barbed-wire fence. He did it with His love, grace, mercy, and *His people*. A Jesus-loving community saved our marriage and brought His love and support just when we needed it.

You cannot overcome the desert or wilderness seasons of your life alone.

Our level of need was great, but God's love was greater.

God always provides where He guides.

He provided His love and His support for us through *His people*.

I'm certain this is His plan for you too.

"We are created for community, fashioned for fellowship, and formed for a family, and none of us can fulfill God's purposes by ourselves."[4]

- **Rick Warren**

---

[4] Warren, R. (2012). *The purpose driven life: What on earth am I here for?* Zondervan, p 74.

CHAPTER NINE

CHURCH HURT AND THE FEAR OF MAN

> *"For we speak as messengers approved by God to be entrusted with the Good News. Our purpose is to please God, not people. He alone examines the motives of our hearts."*
>
> **1 Thessalonians 2:4 NLT**

Just because my prison sentence ended, it didn't mean the pain of my past was behind me. I was loved and forgiven by God, my husband, and many important people in my life. To my great dismay, the rest of the world would not see me in the way God did.

I wanted to be accepted as the woman God had transformed and forgiven. I desired to be loved, respected, and valued despite my failures. I wanted people to see and know not just the shiny, easy-to-love parts, but also the dark, ugly, sinful, flawed parts that helped to shape the healed, redeemed woman I am today.

Over the years, I have experienced a lot of rejection and judgment. It's been a hard road for my whole family. My past hasn't just impacted *my* present; it has been a constant toll on both my husband and my children due to persecution from other people. The enemy has spoken through one person after another, attempting to put my sin on display and remind me of what I did.

Piercing, judgmental eyes. Attacks on social media. Anonymous phone calls. Emails to people who have supported me about how evil they are for associating with me. Anxious words of death, gossip, and condemnation would suffocate God's voice and bind me in fear. I spent years fighting the enemy piling on shame in my head, and then, to add insult to injury, the words of people all around me agreeing with him. I did two and a half years in prison and took responsibility for my actions. I repented with God and others. I did years of Christian counseling, Bible studies, and hard soul work. Even still, at times it has felt like a life sentence of being shamed, judged, and rejected no matter how much fruit has bloomed in my life.

Decades had passed, yet still I heard the voices:

"I don't have enough faith that you have changed, Jaymee."

"Jaymee, I cannot work as your photographer because if people learn about your past, they will tie my reputation to yours."

"Jaymee, we would have loved to have you as a guest speaker, but what if people Googled you? We can't take that chance."

"Jaymee, you are qualified for this position in every way, and I know this happened a long time ago, but if our clients found out about your past, we would lose their business."

"Jaymee, our organization is a Christian organization, and we do not want people like you working out here."

"Jaymee, although you are very qualified and have exemplified exceptional character in every area that you have served, we can't hire you. There's a chance that if people found out about your past that we would be canceled."

Disapproval. Rejection. Condemnation. Fear of what culture thinks. Fear of what others think. The enemy replayed his tape over and over in my head, and people cosigned on all his lies. Essentially, the message was this: "Jaymee, your past has disqualified you, and we don't want to tie our business, ministry, or organization to you because *of how people will view us* if we do."

This scarlet letter has been tattooed to a pseudoidentity, one that would destroy my life all over again with shame if I chose to step into it. I could write story after story of some unimaginable things people have said and done to me, my family, and my friends because of that stain. One would think that this is a natural and expected response from unbelievers and the world, but what about other followers of Jesus?

Every statement you read above was spoken to me by people who say they love Jesus and identify themselves as Christians.

About a year ago, my husband and I were sitting in a large church community of married couples, and the pastor leading that night began to talk about the Apostle Paul and his tainted past. I always love hearing people preach about Paul, because I resonate in many ways with Paul's redemption story. However, the message took a turn that I was not anticipating.

The pastor began to talk about Paul's past and his notorious rap sheet before meeting Jesus on the road to Damascus. The words that came out of his mouth next made my heart sink to the floor.

Laughing he said, "If Paul attended our church today, he wouldn't have even been able to serve or volunteer here!" He continued to chuckle as many people in the audience joined his unintentional self-righteousness. As a baby Christian, I might have walked out of the room. I'm pretty sure Jesus and I both had the same reaction.

Indignation.
Sorrow.
Heartbreak.

I wasn't offended personally by the comment and laughter, because God had done a work in establishing my worth and identity in Christ. But I pictured the man or woman in that room that may not even be a believer that was carrying the shame of "larger sins," "worse sins," or "scarlet letter sins." Can you imagine how they felt?

This church was missing Christ and His mercy. Their laughter revealed a subtle wave of self-righteousness, fear, and pride woven into the body of Christ.

I have a mentor, Susie, who says it this way, "We are to always love the sinner, and hate our sin more than someone else's." Is it showing love and mercy to laugh about someone's "disqualifying past"? Have we quickly forgotten our own wretchedness that Jesus died for? A sobering question: could Paul, David, or Jaymee serve, pastor, speak, lead, and volunteer at your church?

The answer to that question across American churches tells us a great deal about the American church and who we have put our faith in: Jesus or platform? Jesus or followers on social media? Jesus or public opinion? Jesus or our reputation? Jesus or fear of man?

> *Father, forgive them, for they know not what they do. Father, forgive them, because the church is full of sinners just like me. Lord, thank you that despite human frailty, your grace cannot be stopped. The faithfulness and sovereignty of God are not deterred because of the Church's fear of man.*

"Fear of man" is a Biblical concept that refers to an *excessive worry* about what other people think, say, or do, leading to a dependence on the approval of others and a neglect of God's will. It can manifest as anxiety, insecurity, and a reluctance to act according to one's convictions. It can also show up as judgment and pride. These people who judged and rejected me weren't afraid of *me*… they were afraid of what other people would think of their association with me. The more I endured, the more I realized it wasn't really about me at all.

After facing these accusing voices for many years, I came to recognize that the words they spoke to me or about my past were more about their own fear, lack of faith, or judgmental spirit rather than about my identity in Christ. Once the Holy Spirit revealed this, everything changed for me. I didn't have to walk around feeling less than, unworthy, rejected, or offended. A new boldness arose. I began seeing everyone who spoke death over me or who caved to the fear of man as simply another person who needed their own healing journey.

God uses these things for our protection or redirection, and I have learned to trust Him despite the Church and its shortcomings.

I got to the point that when someone threw my past in my face, I would share my testimony with two new people. I wasn't trying to hide my past. I was obediently sharing Christ's triumph *over* my past. My story is not a story of shame; it is a story of redemption. I was not going to be silenced by the enemy anymore. I knew who I was in Christ, and no one could ever take that away from me. I longed to bring hope to many who were lost or entangled in the shame of their own sin. My testimony is a message of freedom that many need to hear, and I knew it was part of my mission in the world to share it. My testimony is evidence for the *gospel*.

> *"But in your hearts revere Christ as Lord. Always be prepared to give an answer to everyone who asks you to give the reason for the hope that you have. But do this with gentleness and respect."*
>
> **1 Peter 3:15 NIV**

We must stop allowing the enemy to silence us from sharing where our hope comes from. Jesus transforms. Jesus heals and turns the most broken parts of us into wholeness in Him. So many people are lost, broken, and hurting, and they need to hear our redemption stories. Without the hope of Jesus, all we have is despair or a false sense of security, pride, and self-sufficiency. A hope built on sinking sand is no hope at all.

The Church let me down. It caused me to question if the people in our congregations truly believe in the working power of the gospel. It caused me to wonder if people still believe in transformation through Christ. It wounded me in a way I would not easily recover from.

And yet, I knew I needed the Church. Despite all the flaws and faults, a church is an essential community for followers of Jesus. Many believers will not stay and trust God when they have been hurt by the church. They walk away angry, wounded, offended, and bitter. Ministry is messy. The church is not perfect. I refused to take the bait of the enemy to stay angry and bitter. I have learned that the only way through these messy imperfections is to forgive, offer grace, and have humble, hard conversations. To surrender, forgive, and trust God to use it for good. *He is faithful.* And finally, to pray for those who persecute.

To anyone who has experienced wounds from the Church, I get it. It hurts. I'm not denying the pain, I am inviting you to welcome God into it and respond in a way that honors Christ despite your feelings. If we are going to participate in the healing of the Church, we must stop gossiping and complaining, and start praying. We need to turn to Christ and work towards unity, reconciliation, and healing.

Of course, there are situations of spiritual abuse or false teaching where God will lead us to leave a particular church. However, more often than not, the reality is that the Church is full of sinners and broken people trying to become more like Jesus. We don't always get it right. And the by-product of this brings betrayal, rejection, and hurt. We have *a choice* to stay in our offense and bitterness or to forgive, wrestle through the "hard", and walk out these relationships in a way that honors Christ. It's an opportunity for all parties to grow and mature, and I am grateful for the perspective that my pain has given me.

I love the church. I've been leading and serving in the church for over 20 years. I love my brothers and sisters in Christ, yet I will not sit back idly and pretend that succumbing to the fear of man is ok. God is not pleased with it, and so with great love and humility, I'm calling us out. When we know better, we must do better.

Church, we are called to grow in maturity and discernment. We must ask ourselves: do we fear man more than we fear the Lord? Too often, the fear of judgment—or the concern for how others may perceive us—keeps us silent. Silent when we should proclaim the truth. Silent when we should testify to the power of the gospel through transformed lives.

When reputation becomes more important than obedience and conviction, the witness of the gospel is diminished. Instead, we are called to walk in courage, to walk in humility, and to walk in trust—trusting that the God who builds His church will also defend and protect it. He is faithful. And He is seeking a church that will not shrink back but will lift high the name of Jesus no matter the cost.

That cost may be real. It may mean members walking away. Donors withholding support. Being "cancelled" on social media. Personal attacks, criticism, judgment, hatred. The loss of property. Intense and unprecedented spiritual warfare. And if we imagine Jesus alive in our cultural moment, He would endure all these things—and more.

So, the question remains: do we have this kind of fear of the Lord?

May we, His church, be fortified not to seek the approval of man, but to long for this—

- to see souls saved,
- to see captives set free,
- to see lives forever transformed by the power of the gospel of Jesus Christ.

Let us be a church saturated in love and compassion, yet bold in proclaiming truth—no matter the cost

> *"The LORD is for me, so I will have no fear. What can mere people do to me?"*
>
> **Psalm 118:16 (NLT)**

Recently I experienced a pastor who stood up to the fear of man because he knew that the hope my testimony brought was far more important than his reputation.

Pastor Stephan was leading a small church of about 50 young adults in their 20s and 30s. Many of them were brand-new believers. He called me on a Monday and said, "Hey, I've been praying about this, and I feel the Lord is leading me to have you come and share your testimony this coming Friday."

I was immediately anxious. At this time, I had never shared my testimony publicly nor with any strangers. God had, over the years, aligned me with dozens of divine appointments to share with people I had relationship with. Everyone close to me or who worked with me in ministry knew my story. I was comfortable sharing in those spaces. But these were all *strangers*.

The other part of my anxiety was that I had four days to prepare. Your girl is a reformed type A perfectionist type, and so at first, I wanted to say no. Of course, the Holy Spirit was all over me saying, *"Jaymee, say yes, and trust me."*

I was used to being in front of a crowd, teaching and speaking. I was *made to do this* for the glory of God. Yet this was different. I wanted to throw up. I wanted to run as I pictured people preparing to stone me like the woman caught in adultery. My heart was ready to jump out of my chest as I walked up to that mic and looked into an abyss of unfamiliar eyes. I had a few of my friends in the audience, so I smiled at them nervously and, with sweaty palms, I took a deep breath.

The Holy Spirit changed my opening statement in a matter of seconds. I said, "Before I share my testimony, I want to address three different groups of people. First, to those of you who have felt so much guilt, shame, or regret for something you have done. I believe God brought you here to set you free from those snares. God wants you to know you are forgiven and loved and that your sin does not define you. God does not want you suffocating in shame anymore. Second, by the grace of God, some of you might not have had too much suffering in your lives. For the most part, you have stayed on the narrow road of following Jesus up to this point. No major failures or detours into the enemy's clutches. No major traumas to derail your life. For you, this story will most certainly challenge your walk and hopefully stir your faith. It may expose some self-righteousness and pride. I would ask you to see me and this story through the eyes of Jesus, and that God may use it to equip you to walk alongside someone who has really blown it. And thirdly, due to the heaviness of the sin story in my testimony, there may be some of you who are triggered due to your healing journey. Please know you have full permission to get up and leave without judgment."

The Holy Spirit took over with great boldness, earnestness, and authenticity. I was probably one of the most unpolished speakers you ever heard, but there was no doubt that the Living God had entered that room and was working in the hearts of the people.

God was setting the captives free.
He was offering them hope.
He was igniting their faith.
He was drawing them into deeper wells of healing with their Savior.

After I finished speaking, I had a line of about 15 women in tears wanting to talk to me. One after another, they asked, "How do you share your testimony without shame or fear of judgement? I want to share my testimony, but I am so afraid of how people will respond. Thank you so much for being so courageous today."

One person's courage opens the door for someone else to be brave. Hell is so afraid of our testimonies. Not the *safe* testimony; the *vulnerable* one.

A young man who was about 28 or 30 years old walked up to me. His eyes were full of tears. He said, "I wasn't going to come today. I had given up on God. My mom has been an addict for most of my life, and no matter how much I prayed, she has never gotten better. A friend invited me tonight and said, 'You have to come and hear a powerful testimony.'"

He said he reluctantly agreed, but knew as soon as I started speaking that God had brought me there for him. He continued, "You were in prison *with my mom*, Ms. Jaymee. I couldn't believe it when you started sharing the location and timeline. My hope has been renewed that if God can transform your life the way He did, I know He can transform and heal my mom too!"

I was undone.

Tears were streaming down both our cheeks as I hugged him.

Heaven was celebrating, and the gates of hell were shaking.

The Lord was not done showing His power and mercy. We moved into a time of prayer in groups of four, based on where we were sitting. As the worship music played in the background, three women scooted their chairs towards us to make a very close circle. One by one, they talked for the first time about being sexually abused or assaulted. With the utmost bravery, tears rolling down their cheeks, obliterating the darkness and kicking shame in the teeth, they shared their stories.

    I sat there bawling with three strangers.
    Sweet daughters of the King of Kings.
    There was no "surface" or "fake" in that room.
    No pretending to be fine.
    No fear.
    Just the darkness being brought to the light.
    Just the healing touch of Jesus.
    It was a breath of heaven blowing through that room.

What if every church service were like this? I couldn't help but dream of seeing men and women in a large sanctuary at the altar crying out to God and then surrounded by other believers in prayer, sharing their darkest secrets *safely*. The Spirit of God wrecking everyone in the best way. Where great sin abounds, God's grace and power abound even greater.

This is what the Church is meant to be: an embodiment of Christ's love, forgiveness, grace, and truth. A place where people can confess their sin and be embraced in a way that leads them to repentance, transformation, and wholeness. I pray every church in America can have the same courage that this pastor had to allow the unspeakable, tainted, scarlet letter testimonies shatter the darkness. This is the heart of the gospel.

Back in 2012, a million-dollar franchise gym chain that I worked for had seven different locations in the area shortly after I came home from prison. A disgruntled staff member, angry about schedule changes, found out about my past and used my background as a means to attack the company. This staff member had also threatened to expose my past to the news media, even though nothing illegal had occurred at the gym, nor had I violated any kind of company etiquette.

I was called down to corporate to speak with the CEO and Vice President, thinking I was getting a promotion or another teaching opportunity. I soon discovered that, when I was hired, the branch I worked for didn't do a background check. The hiring manager was aware of my background, but she didn't follow all the procedures. I braced myself for the waves of judgement, shame, and condemnation.

Instead, I received favor. I will never forget how professionally the CEO and VP handled the situation. God opened the door for me to share my story and share the gospel. The VP had tears in her eyes. They looked at each other and thanked me for my complete honesty. She said, "You know, Jaymee, everyone has a past, and I am inspired by how you haven't allowed your mistakes to define you. We believe in second chances, and I am amazed at how you have bounced back despite all that you have been through. You are an extraordinary instructor and employee. We are grateful for the way you connect with members and how you use your talents to help others prioritize their health. In the few years you have worked for our organization you have been nothing but professional. We are going to stand behind you. I actually would like you to travel to some of our other locations and teach some masterclass workshops for twice your normal pay."

This is called the favor and protection of God. What the enemy meant to destroy me, God used for my good. And in this case, neither the company nor its leaders were Christians. Where most people saw humiliation or loss, God made an opportunity for me to share the gospel.

If you have ever felt dismissed, rejected, overlooked, or condemned because of your past, please stand on this scripture:

> *For God knew his people in advance, and he chose them to become like his Son so that his Son would be the firstborn among many brothers and sisters. And having chosen them, he called them to come to him. And having called them, he*

gave them right standing with himself. And having given them right standing, he gave them his glory.

What shall we say about such wonderful things as these? If God is for us, who can ever be against us? Since he did not spare even his own Son but gave him up for us all, won't he also give us everything else? Who dares accuse us whom God has chosen for his own? No one—for God himself has given us the right to stand with Himself. Who then will condemn us? No one—for Christ Jesus died for us and was raised to life for us, and he is sitting in the place of honor at God's right hand, pleading for us.

Can anything ever separate us from Christ's love? Does it mean he no longer loves us if we have trouble or calamity, or are persecuted, or hungry, or destitute, or in danger, or threatened with death? As the Scriptures say, "For your sake we are killed every day; we are being slaughtered like sheep. No, despite all these things, overwhelming victory is ours through Christ, who loved us.

And I am convinced that nothing can ever separate us from God's love. Neither death nor life, neither angels nor demons, neither our fears for today nor our worries about tomorrow—not even the powers of hell can separate us from God's love. No power in the sky above or the earth below—indeed, nothing in all creation will ever be able to separate us from the love of God that is revealed in Christ Jesus our Lord.

Romans 8:29-39 NLT

When we bow down to the opinions of others, we dishonor our Creator—the One who died for us, chose us, loves us, called us, and will equip us to do His will. It is nothing more than a ploy of the enemy to make us shrink back, silence our testimonies, dim our light, and bury the very gifts and talents God entrusted to us for His glory.

What Jesus is looking for is radical obedience. A holy boldness that says, *I will do what God has called me to do—no matter the cost, no matter the loss.* The fear of man whispers that God's approval and acceptance are not enough. But the truth is, they are the only things that truly matter.

> *"Am I now trying to win the approval of human beings, or of God? Or am I trying to please people? If I were still trying to please people, I would not be a servant of Christ."*
>
> **Galatians 1:10 NIV**

CHAPTER TEN

RESCUED BY GRACE

> *For it is by grace you have been saved, through faith—and this is not from yourselves, it is the gift of God—not by works, so that no one can boast.*
>
> **Ephesians 2: 8-9 NIV**

I wrote this book so that I could share a story of despair turned to hope, darkness turned to light, and brokenness turned to redemption. This is my story, and I am eternally grateful for the opportunity to tell it. Now, I want to share the most important piece of my journey. If it were not for this chapter of my tale, I wouldn't be able to share any lasting hope or light or redemption with anyone. Jesus made all the difference in my life, and it is because of Him that I have found freedom, truth, and life made new. This is my story of being rescued by grace.

Some people reject Christianity, but the things they reject are not an accurate representation of what genuine Christians believe, nor are they an accurate reflection of who Jesus is. On the other hand, people are walking around proclaiming that they are Christians, yet the way they talk and live does not align with Jesus or the Bible.

I was this person.

For 26 years of my life, I claimed to be a Christian because I believed in God, but the truth was I was completely lost. I was following Jaymee's plan for her life, not God's, until one day, I made a decision that would change my life forever.

One Sunday in early August of 2005, a 6'4", linebacker-looking man named RV Brown approached the pulpit at our church. RV's biceps were as big as my head, and he looked like he could probably get people to surrender their lives to Jesus by putting a WWF wrestling move on them. I bet in his prime, he would have given "The Rock " a run for his money. He was a big dude!

The tone of RV's voice was equally as intimidating as his physical presence. He sounded like a hybrid of James Earl Jones and Martin Luther King Jr. The moment he began speaking, not a single person was dozing as he paced back and forth on the stage like he was sizing us up. His dark brown eyes were intense and passionate, and his voice brought a genuine conviction as it bellowed the gospel message. My heart was pounding, my eyes were flooded, and I knew God was speaking to me that day. For weeks, I had been slowly surrendering. I finally understood for the first time that God was personal, and speaking directly to me week after week at church.

But today was different.

The Holy Spirit would use RV to call me to *a full surrender*. I realized that although I had called myself a Christian my entire life, I did not have an understanding of what it meant to be a follower of Jesus. I was not saved. I was perishing on earth and eternally, and I didn't even know it. If I had died that day, I was not going to heaven.

I knew about God. I believed God existed. However, I most certainly did not have an accurate understanding of the gospel or Jesus, nor did I see how my wretchedness needed a Savior.

The good news that Jesus offered was there for the receiving. God had been pursuing me my whole life, present and waiting, loving me through my shame. In order to receive His forgiveness and experience His redemption in my life, there were some essential understandings that I had to embrace.

I needed to admit I was a sinner.

I needed to admit I needed a Savior.

I needed to acknowledge that up to that point, I had been trying to do things my way.

I needed to admit I was broken.

I needed to admit I needed God's forgiveness.

As I listened to RV that day, I came to understand that becoming a Christian wasn't about earning my way to heaven through achievement. I had been carrying around this idea that if the good things I did on earth outweighed the bad things, then God and I were good. I was a pretty "good" person compared to most people, right? Surely this would get me a ticket to pass through the pearly gates on judgment day, right?

I believed that my "works" would save me.

Do more good than bad.

Follow the Ten Commandments.

Go through confirmation in the Catholic Church.

Get baptized as a baby.

Feed the poor.

Serve at church

Read my Bible.

Go through all the rituals.

Be a good rule follower.

Compare my life to others instead of to Jesus.

Work or achieve my way to heaven.

Finally, I realized the truth. The fruit of good works is a result of our faith. Jesus tells us it's not the good works that lead to salvation. If I truly believe that Jesus is my Lord, and that He is the only one who can save me from my sin, there will be evidence in my life that reflects His redemption. But my measure of goodness could never compare *to Jesus' perfection.*

On my own, I was not "good enough" for heaven.

There is not one human on the face of this earth capable of earning our own way to salvation. There is not one of us who is perfect or without sin. That's why God came down himself as Jesus, because only someone perfect could atone for all of mankind's sins. When we come into a personal relationship with Jesus, God sees Jesus instead of our sins. We are made right because of Him, not through all that we have done or achieved in terms of "good works".

RV shared the passage from Ephesians that made it clear to me.

> *"For it is **by grace** you have been saved, **through faith**—and this is **not from yourselves**, it is the gift of God— **not by works** so that no one can boast.*
>
> **Ephesians 2:8-9 NIV**

Up until that point, I wanted to be saved from hell, but I didn't want to be saved from the hell inside of me. I wanted a free ticket to heaven, but I didn't want to surrender control of my life to God. That day, I heard the truth:

Humble yourself.
Surrender.
Admit you need God.
Decide to turn away from your plan and follow God's instead.

It was becoming clear to me as I allowed my pride and strength to release into surrender and humility. I can't change myself. I can't fix myself. Only the supernatural power of God can transform me. God simply required my surrender and a desire to seek Him with all of my heart, mind, and soul. He required me to have faith and to believe that He is who He says He is, and that He will do what He said He would do.

There I sat with RV, bringing to light that I was a sinner who was in desperate need of a Savior. I was sitting with my husband just four rows back from the front of the pulpit.

RV said, "Now, I'm going to ask some of you to be bold publicly. You know God is knocking on the door of your heart, and you know that everything I said was God speaking directly to you. You *know you have heard the truth, and you now know the truth.* If that is you, I want you to walk up to this stage right now."

Oh, man. I already was feeling all the conviction internally, and now God wanted me to let all three hundred people in the room know, too.

I looked at my husband with tears in my eyes and nodded my head. "Let's go."

We held hands as we walked up to the altar, where the 6'4" man had crouched down to get close to us. I could sense the smiles and joy of all the other Christians in the room, anticipating what was about to happen. There were about thirty of us standing there together, with rays of light from the stage billowing down on us like heaven had just opened for this moment.

Ever so softly and gently, RV asked us to raise our hands as he prayed. He looked me straight in the eyes, giving me an affirming nod and a smile of approval that I had never gotten from my dad.

He looked at me and said, "Sweet daughter, don't cry. It's ok. Jesus has been waiting for this moment your whole life. Heaven is celebrating with us."

My chest was violently shaking as I felt the presence of God overcome me.

His warmth engulfed my heart.

His love embraced me.

His forgiveness covered me.

It was like all the weight I had carried in my soul was being lifted. You don't realize the weight of 2000 tons until it's gone. All the sin, all the shame, all the rejection, all the bitterness, all the mud that had buried my heart was about to be washed clean, as white as snow. I prayed with every part of me, and for the first time, I completely surrendered.

I accepted Jesus as my Lord and Savior that day. I repented of all my sins and asked God for forgiveness. I decided to give up my own way of living. I wanted a fresh start with Jesus.

> *If you declare with your mouth, "Jesus is Lord," and believe in your heart that God raised him from the dead, you will be saved. ¹⁰ For it is with your heart that you believe and are justified, and it is with your mouth that you profess your faith and are saved.*
>
> **Romans 10:9-10 NIV**

That was the day I became a Christian. A *real Jesus Christ follower*.

In this holy moment, all was made new. And even better was the miracle that my husband and I got saved at the same time, on the same day! When Craig and I put our trust in Jesus that day, everything changed. August 2005 not only changed the trajectory of our lives, but also our kids, our grandkids, and the generations to come.

Heaven was roaring. I was rescued by the loving grace of God. Not because I was worthy by my actions, but because I belonged to Him. I am worthy because I was created by Him and for Him.

Jesus looked into that crowd and said, *"I want her, that one, right there! Fear not, Jaymee, for I have redeemed you; I have called you by name, you are mine."*

> *Where sin increased, grace increased all the more, so that, just as sin reigned in death, so also grace might reign through righteousness to bring eternal life through Jesus Christ our Lord.*
>
> **Romans 5:20b-21 NIV**

One decision.

It was a complete surrender of my will.
Not my will be done, but your will alone, God. That's what I want.

> " In the same way, there is more joy in heaven over one lost sinner who repents and returns to God than over ninety-nine others who are righteous and haven't strayed away!"
>
> **Luke 15:7 NLT**

Hell was enraged.
We had passed from spiritual death to spiritual life.
We became citizens of heaven.
We were reconciled by Jesus' death on the cross.
We were sealed with the Holy Spirit.

Our salvation was secure; no one could take it away from us. We had access to God's peace that would guard our hearts. Our names were written in the Book of Life. We got to begin a close, intimate fellowship with the Father, Son, and Holy Spirit. The Holy Spirit dwelt inside of us to teach us what is true and expose lies we believed. We were now co-laborers with Christ to spread the gospel and strengthen the faith of other believers.

What about you?

Whether you know Jesus or not, He delights in you, He wants to spend time with you, and He sees you just as you are: every gift, every strength, every flaw, every dark secret, every insecurity, every failure, and He loves you just the same.

> "So, as the Holy Spirit says: 'Today, if you hear his voice, do not harden your hearts as you did in the rebellion, during the time of testing in the wilderness.'"

Hebrews 3:7-8 NIV

Perhaps today, you need to surrender, repent, and call on the name of Jesus for the first time. Turn to God and declare Jesus Christ as your Lord and Savior, not just with your words, but also with your heart. **Believe!**

Perhaps today, you know Jesus, but you have walked away for a season, trying to do things your way and in your strength. You know your life isn't aligning with God's will. You are saved, but you need to repent and come back to God. **Repent!**

Perhaps today, you know Jesus and have a genuine relationship, but you are either stuck in some sin patterns, or you are apathetic and stagnant in your faith. You are intentional in following Jesus in every way you know how, but you know God has more for you. Pray. Fast. Cry out to God! Keep reading, God has new levels of His intimacy and freedom waiting. Ask the Holy Spirit! **Seek!**

> *"If we confess our sins, he is faithful and just and will forgive us our sins and purify us from all unrighteousness."*
>
> **1 John 1:9 NIV**

God had so much work to do in me after this salvation moment! This was only the beginning. I had so much baggage still in my soul that needed the healing, delivering power of Jesus. It wasn't about achieving perfection in that moment, but rather embracing a lifetime of transformation through the work of the Holy Spirit.

When we receive the gift of salvation, we also receive the gift of the Holy Spirit, and the Spirit of God begins to transform and change us from the inside out. We then have a desire to read the Bible, get into a Christian community, pray, and seek to spend time in the presence of God and His people. Jesus was meeting me right where I was, but He had no intention of keeping me the same person. When you have a legit encounter and surrender to the will of the Almighty Living God, YOU WILL NEVER BE THE SAME AGAIN!

>You are loved.
>You are forgiven.
>You are cherished.
>You are worthy.
>You are God's masterpiece.
>You have a purpose.
>You are beautiful just the way He created you.
>You are accepted.
>You are made new.
>You are strong.
>You are radiant.
>You are an overcomer.
>You are a miracle.
>You are blessed.
>You are a warrior.
>You are a child of God.
>You are HIS.

> *"Here I am! I stand at the door and knock. If anyone hears my voice and opens the door, I will come in and eat with that person, and they with me."*
>
> **Revelation 3:20 NIV**

EPILOGUE

FINISHING THE RACE WITH RESILIENCE

Let us not become weary in doing good, for at the proper time we will reap a harvest if we do not give up. Therefore, as we have the opportunity, let us do good to all people, especially to those who belong to the family of believers.

Galatians 6:9-10 NIV

In full transparency, I finished the initial manuscript of this book in May of 2024. The summer was dedicated to the final editing and publishing that fall. My summer plans were to be full of relaxing beach trips, a shift from our family's busy schedules, more intentional sabbath time, more aimless shopping trips through Ross, more family memories, and the final touches to this book. Yet God once again had a different plan.

> *"Jaymee, much of what you have written in this book has been to testify about what I have done in your life in the past. Suffering in your past had to do with a lot of the consequences of your sin and rebellion. I want you to revise this last chapter. It will be drenched with what I am doing in your life right now as you suffer well to finish this assignment."*

Here's the truth: I still fall short and sin daily; just ask my husband and my kids. Yet there's a difference between blatantly sinning and knowingly living in disobedience versus faithfully choosing to serve and follow Jesus with a desire to obey Him in all you do, repenting daily for the places you fall short.

Yet even if you fall into the latter category, guess what? *Seasons of suffering still come.*

I have had my share of suffering in this life. Some as consequences of my own sin, some as the reality of living in a broken world, and some because of my *obedience to the assignment to share my story.* I remember sitting with a friend recently as tears just spilled over my coffee cup. I bowed my head in trust and submission to God's plan in this season as she prayed 1 Peter 5:10 over me:

"Jaymee, after you have suffered a little while, the God of grace who has called you to His eternal glory in Christ, will Himself restore, confirm, strengthen, and establish you."

God has a plan to use the suffering we endure for our good and the good of others. Why? Because sadly, our human nature does not typically need God, until God is all we have. In our comforts, successes, and self-sufficiency, we typically put God on a shelf until crisis, until failure, until desperation, *until suffering.*

Surely suffering makes sense when you are in rebellion against God's will for your life. Suffering and pain are natural consequences of disobedience. What about attacks, suffering, and pain when you are serving and obeying God in every way you know possible? Sometimes it seems that the more you obey and walk out your assignment, the *more you get attacked?*

This season has been a tsunami of suffering for me.

I have experienced multiple days of not being able to catch my breath, feeling like I was drowning. Wave after wave, the enemy has launched a full arsenal of war against me from every angle possible. I have wanted to quit writing this book about every other day this summer. I find myself on my knees wiping up snot and tear puddles more than anything else.

At first, I was full steam ahead, I was full of zeal, joy, and excitement for the assignment. I couldn't wait to write the book after God placed it in a vision 15 years ago.

I remember when the dream was first planted in my heart. I was in prison at a prayer shut-in with all my sisters in Christ in blue. For seven hours we praised, prayed, and wept in a little chapel in the prison yard. No "freedom", no food; we just wanted Jesus. It was one of the most powerful and beautiful times of worship in my entire life. The brokenness and humility in that room ushered in the full presence of the almighty God. It was in that little chapel in April of 2008 that God gave me a vivid prophetic vision of me standing with a microphone in one hand and a book in my other hand. The Holy Spirit said, *"Jaymee, one day you will be a messenger of hope to use your testimony to lead many people to Christ and set people free."*

The irony! I am in prison, and you have called *me* to set the captives free?

Do you know exactly 15 years later *to the day* of that vision, a board room of a ministry I worked for heard from God and said, "It's time for Jaymee to write her book and share her story."

This is our God!

How could I not be excited to write this book! But ever since that decision in the board room, there has been an opposition in the spiritual realms to force my silence and defeat.

Intense long-suffering would ensue.

God didn't cause the suffering, but He has allowed the suffering to happen to be a tool to get me to a place spiritually where my walk with Him cannot be shaken. The suffering is to chip off any sin or flesh that is still trying to hold on. Like a chisel on a sculpture to conform me and mold me into being more like Jesus.

This process hurts.
It is not for the faint of heart.

It's a spiritual warfare boot camp. Satan sees defeat. God sees opportunity. God uses our suffering to create warriors that draw from His strength. Within the trials, fires, valleys, and deserts, He equips and strengthens us to overcome and be victorious. Our victory means hope and victory for others. Instead of our life being a message of despair or self-centeredness, it becomes a message of hope to a hurt, lost, and broken world.

We cry out in the fire, "Why is this happening? When will the suffering end?"

Psalm 13:1-4 was on repeat for me:

> *"How long, O lord? Will you forget me forever? How long will you hide your face from me? How long must I wrestle with my thoughts and day after day have sorrow in my heart? How long will my enemy triumph over me? Look on me and answer, Lord my God. Give light to my eyes, or I will sleep in death, and my enemy will say, "I have overcome him," and my foes will rejoice when I fall."*
>
> **Psalm 13:1-4 NIV**

It felt like six months of being *crushed*.

My sister died.

My mom went into depression and is now physically crippled.

I lost my job.

Debilitating chronic pain escalated in my back and hips to where there are days I cannot even walk.

A seemingly random social media and public spectacle attack was launched on my reputation, my church, and my ministry due to my past.

My son experienced cyberbullying and constant harassment because of my past.

We continued the hard work of health in the family dynamics of our home and marriage.

We lived through another round of false accusations, slander, and gossip within a professional circle.

Two weeks after I finished the first manuscript of this book, a sudden health diagnosis taunted the ugly word *cancer* at my left breast and uterus.

My 10-year-old daughter was in a horrible bicycle accident where half her face got peeled off like a banana and I had to feed her through a syringe for a week. In addition to her badly injured face, she had road rash, a broken tooth, and all the pain to go with it. We almost had to hospitalize her due to dehydration.

A few weeks later, my son was hit by someone driving 50 mph, full speed, after running a red light. His car was totaled and by the grace of God, he walked away from the accident alive. Before he blacked out, he said he felt God's peace all around Him and knew that if he died, he would be in heaven. He went to physical therapy for months to recover from herniated discs in his back and neck.

A few weeks later, my mom took a major fall, breaking her femur, which led to an emergency surgery. We thought we were going to lose her. I am her sole caretaker and am responsible for all her needs. During her healing process and therapy, *she fell again,* resulting in lacerations and slowing down her rehab.

Then, to top it all off, both of my kids got COVID for the first time with the longest days of fevers and difficulty sleeping from coughing that they have ever had.

Six months of *hell* is what I signed up for when I obeyed God's call to write this book.

Yet Jesus faithfully used such suffering to draw me into greater intimacy with Him.
His presence.
His stillness.
His comfort.
His love and softness filling my heart to press on, to keep going.

The whispers of God would come in my quiet time:
"What am I teaching you?
How am I preparing you?
Who will you help and comfort because you have suffered and been comforted?
Where do you need to be humbled?
Where are you still relying on your own strength?
Will you still trust me, Jaymee?"

In the same Psalm 13 David ends with:

> *"But I trust in your unfailing love; my heart rejoices in your salvation. I will sing the Lord's praise, for he has been good to me."*

Psalm 13:5-6 NIV

In suffering, I will still choose to trust.

I will remember my salvation and the first day I met Christ and was filled with His forgiveness, love, grace, and mercy. I will sing to Jesus because I remember all the times He has been good to me and been faithful. Why would He give up on me now?

This season of suffering has taught me that any success I have had or will have is only by the grace of God. There is no room to glorify Jaymee. The space is being created and preserved to GLORIFY GOD.

Through this process, Jaymee has wanted to tap out. Jaymee has been ready to quit. Jaymee has been buried in tears and anguish for months, weeks, and days: crying, praying, praising, yelling, violently weeping. Jaymee has been clinging to her life raft, Jesus, as each wave crashes on her, one after another. Jaymee has been feeling like she was drowning. Jaymee has wondered if the calling God put on her life has been too much to bear. Too overwhelming. Too high a cost.

I've had those moments where I am just done. I think sitting on a beach reading books and working as a barista asking people if they want one cream or two is a more appealing plan. Beach. Sunshine. Books. Coffee. Comfort. *Sign me up.* I quit, God. I'm sorry. Find someone else.

But I can feel Jesus gently touching my cheeks, plump with perimenopause bloat and streams of weary tears. He whispers, *"Daughter, you don't get to choose your calling. Do you really want to be like Jonah? You can run towards what you think would be more comfortable and easy, but at the end of the day, you are going to be shipwrecked, in the belly of a whale, repenting, and back in Nineveh. Instead, trust Me. Lean on Me. This season of suffering will not be wasted."*

So, here I sit in the middle of it. The anointing, the calling, *the crushing.*

Talk about warfare.
Talk about trying not to grow weary in doing good.
This is a crushing for the glory of God.

The enemy only attacks what he is threatened by. If he can't get you to blatantly sin, he will try to distract you, discourage you, and derail you off your assignment. The weapons may be forged, but they will not prosper!

As a Jesus Christ follower, it's like warrior training to be able to better take down the enemy and intercede against his schemes. God builds our faith muscles during these times of warfare so we can sharpen our spiritual weapons that turn us into powerhouses for the kingdom! This is God's promise when we respond well to the suffering.

> I can't give up.
> You can't give up.
> We can't give up.

This race God has called us to run takes great *resilience*. Resilience means the capacity to withstand or to recover quickly from difficulties. It's toughness. It's the ability to endure and last. It means to have a backbone, and to persevere.

It's tenacity.

It's falling seven times and getting back up eight.

It's refusing to bow down to fear, insecurity, failure, or despair.

It's a stripping of every prideful thread in our soul.

It's a determination to stay the course.

Martin Luther King, Jr. said, "If you can't fly then run, if you can't run then walk, if you can't walk then crawl, but whatever you do you have to keep moving forward."[5]

We fall, we get attacked, we fail, but we become stronger because of it. Not because we are strong,

but because Jesus is. We don't cave or give up or wallow in self-pity and bitterness. We cling to Jesus

and move forward with His strength because we know that someone else will come to know Jesus or

get set free because of our commitment to Him. We tarry in prayer with our brothers and sisters in Christ because we can't run this race alone.

---

[5] *April 1969 speech at Spelman College*

We need our people.
We need their encouragement.
We need them to remind us of God's promises.
We need their accountability.
We need their intercession.

Our resilience has eternal ramifications.

May we embrace the magnitude of our "Yes, Lord, send me." We were not placed on this earth by chance. Our assignments from God are the very reason we are here—the sacred purpose for which we were created. And make no mistake: these assignments are not about us. They are about Him. About His glory. About His Kingdom.

Our stories, too, are His.
Every valley of sorrow.
Every scar of shame.
Every victory of grace.
They belong to Him.
They are the ink He uses to write His gospel story on the earth.

And when we steward them well, our testimonies become the most powerful weapon in our hands— for no one can argue with a life transformed.

So I pray, dearest reader, that as you turn these final pages you will no longer hide behind the shadows of defeat or despair. No longer bow to shame. No longer bury your brokenness.

Instead—Rise up.
Lead with your story of redemption.

Lead with your story of hope.

Tell the world how Jesus Christ brought you from death to life. Proclaim how the Living God
took ashes and formed a masterpiece of His grace, His hope, His love. This is how heaven's story advances on earth— through the testimony of His sons and daughters. Through you.

> *"They triumphed over him by the blood of the Lamb and by the word of their testimony; they did not love their lives so much as to shrink from death."*
>
> **Revelation 12:11 NIV**

And for those of you who didn't walk through trauma, chaos, or years of rebellion—do not think you are without a testimony. You, too, carry a grace story. Perhaps your gift from God is that you encountered Jesus early in life, and through His mercy, you remained on the narrow road when countless opportunities to turn away were before you. Yet, you chose Him. Do not minimize this gift. Do not dismiss it as "ordinary." It is the keeping power of God on full display. The world needs to hear that story too—because faithfulness is just as miraculous as deliverance.

What does He want to speak through you?
Write the book.
Start the podcast.
Share on social media.
Take your next step in your healing journey.
Serve where He has assigned you.
Sit at the feet of Jesus and ask Him what He wants you to do in this season.

Your life is a word from the Almighty God to this broken world that *nobody else can speak.*

> "Therefore, since we are surrounded by such a great cloud of witnesses, let us throw off everything that hinders and the sin that so easily entangles. And let us run with perseverance the race marked for us, fixing our eyes on Jesus, the pioneer and perfecter of faith. For the joy set before him he endured the cross, scorning its shame, and sat down at the right hand of the throne of God. Consider him who endured such opposition from sinners, so that you will not grow weary and lose heart."
>
> **Hebrews 12: 1-3 NIV**

One day we will all stand before God and give an account of the "race" we chose to run.

I offer this story in the hope and prayer that I will look into the eyes of Jesus and hear, "Well done my good and faithful servant."

> "I have fought the good fight, I have finished the race, I have kept the faith."
>
> **2 Timothy 4:7 NIV**

ACKNOWLEDGEMENTS
TO A COMMUNITY OF GRACE

> *"A new command I give you: Love one another. As I have loved you, so you must love one another. By this everyone will know that you are my disciples, if you love one another."*
>
> **John 13:34-35 NIV**

Dearest Reader,

I know my acknowledgments section is long for a book of this size and scope. Really long. But I believe it is one of the most important parts of this book.

The story told in the preceding pages is the result of the obedience, love, and faithfulness of the **Body of Christ**. In a culture where so many are walking away from church—or even deconstructing their faith—I want this message to ring loud and clear:

> *It was the love of God, demonstrated through His Church, that made this testimony what it is today.*

Every single person in these acknowledgment pages said "yes" to God and "yes" to loving us. While my name is on the front cover, this book would not exist without the people who came alongside us with discernment, wisdom, support, prayer, longsuffering, encouragement, and love.

So, yes, the acknowledgement section is long, but it matters. Each person deserves to be honored. We all need a godly community around us in order to walk out our divine assignments and fulfill our purpose. We are not made to be alone. Yes, the church can be messy. Yes, it can get ugly at times. But at the end of the day—we are made for communion.

My Lord and Savior Jesus Christ— I thank You with every fiber of my being. Words fall short of capturing the depth of Your love, grace, mercy, and forgiveness. Thank You for never letting go of me—for transforming a story marked by pain, sin, and chaos into a living testimony of hope. Thank You for pursuing me with relentless love and crafting every shattered piece into a radiant mosaic of redemption. Without You, I have nothing; without You, I am nothing. It is only by Your grace that this book has been completed.

May Your name be exalted above every other name. May You be known for who You truly are. I pray your supernatural healing over every reader. I pray you set every captive free from pride, shame, fear, and all that keeps them bound. May their hearts surrender to Your will, finding courage to share their testimonies for Your glory, until the day when every tongue confesses and every knee bows to proclaim that You, Jesus, are the Christ—forever and ever, Amen.

1 Thessalonians 5: 12-13 NIV

> *"Now we ask you, brothers and sisters, to acknowledge those who work hard among you, who care for you in the Lord, and who admonish you. Hold them in the highest regard in love because of their work. Live in peace with each other."*

Ecclesiastes 4:9-10a NIV

> *"Two are better than one, because they have a good return for their labor; if either of them falls down, one can help the other up."*

To my husband, Craig Wallace—

There are no words vast enough to hold my gratitude for you. As Christ, who was fully man and fully God, never gave up on me or on us, so you, too, refused to let go when the storm raged fiercest. You had a thousand reasons to leave, yet you stayed. Our road has been paved with trials, shadows, and seasons that tested the very fabric of our vows. You carried the weight of my mistakes, shouldered shame that was not yours to bear, and endured the whispers and stones thrown by others. Yet through you, God's grace shone like morning light after the darkest night.

You have been my rock when my world crumbled, my anchor when the tide pulled strong, my shelter when the arrows flew. You stood—steadfast, unshaken—when I had no strength left to stand. Your love has been a living sermon of covenant faithfulness, a testimony to the power of denying self in order to trust that our good God could redeem every fragment of our story.

I believe this is only the beginning. God's call on our marriage reaches beyond the pages of this book, into the lives of those who need hope for their own. May our story whisper to weary hearts: *Hold on. God is not finished yet.*

Craig, I love you to heaven and back, to eternity and beyond. Until we meet Jesus face to face, I am—and will always be—your ride-or-die.

To my mother, Yvonne Lane—

Mama, when God chose you to be my mother, He gave me one of His greatest gifts. You have been the steady hand guiding me toward the cross, the voice that prayed heaven open over my life, and the heart that loved me without condition. Because of your love, your prayers, and that single invitation to church, I met Jesus. And because I met Him, my children know Him, and my marriage was saved. Our family's legacy will forever echo in the footsteps of those who follow Christ—because you lit the way.

I know your own story began in hardship, marked by pain and trials few could endure. Yet you rose above the odds, choosing to love more sacrificially than anyone I have ever known. You have given when you had little, served when no one was watching, and carried the burdens of others as if they were your own.

Thank you for caring for Tyson alongside Craig while I was away. Thank you for laying down your comfort so that my little family could stand through the fire. You are noble in spirit, generous in heart, and the hardest worker I know. I have never seen a selfish bone in your body—you poured yourself out until there was nothing left, and then you gave still more.

Mama, I will never know how you did it all as a single mother, but I do know this: heaven has crowns with your name on them. And when you place them at the feet of Jesus, you will realize that sometimes your greatest assignment in life wasn't something you accomplished, but someone you raised. I love you so much, Mom!

To my son, Tyson Isaiah—

It's hard to believe we just dropped you off for your first year in college. From the moment you were born, God used your life as the thread that held Dad and me together through my prison sentence. In those quiet, aching nights, He filled my heart with prayers for you—prayers so fierce they seemed to shake the walls. He whispered promises about your calling, your purpose, and your Kingdom assignment that still leave me in awe. You are a treasure beyond words, and it is one of my life's greatest honors to be your mother.

The weight of our family's testimony has not been light for you to carry. I know the enemy came hard for you, especially in recent years. Yet God will redeem every attack, weaving them into a story so powerful it will change lives. I will never forget your words: *"Mom, there's nothing you could have done that would make me love you any less. You are not that person anymore, and I am proud of how you are using everything you went through to lead people to Jesus."* Those words are carved into my heart forever.

Thank you for walking through the warfare this book stirred and not allowing your faith to be stolen. The dreams and visions He gave me for you in that prison cell will one day burst into reality—and when they do, you will see the fullness of the lion-hearted spirit He's placed within you. Watch, my son. God is about to set your heart ablaze for His glory! You are marked for greatness, Tyson Isaiah!

To my daughter, Trinity Marie—

As I write these words, you are just about to turn twelve. You are joy embodied—God's light wrapped in laughter, love, and life. You are sweet and innocent, yet you carry a wisdom far beyond your years. After much prayer, your dad and I recently shared our testimony with you. It was heavy, and my heart ached knowing you had to process my past and the suffering it carried at such a young age. But I know our God is greater, and I pray that our story will make the gospel come alive to you—that Jesus will be more real to you than ever before.

Even before you knew your mama's full story, God had already placed compassion in your heart for the least of these—for widows, the homeless, the orphaned, and *now the prisoners*. You carry a quiet strength, but you're never afraid to speak when the moment calls for courage. I pray this book helps you walk boldly in who God is and in who He says you are. I pray that every lie of unworthiness shatters, and that you stand rooted in the truth of His healing, transformative power. Always remember—God's word, prayer, Godly community, and surrender are the keys to walking in His purpose for your life! Nothing is too hard for God to redeem, but we must run *to Him*.

Thank you for loving me so deeply and for sacrificing moments with me so I could complete this divine assignment. I cherish the way we finish each other's sentences, the way we laugh until our cheeks hurt, and every single adventure we share. You are a miracle, Trinity—a gift straight from the Father's hands. I am blessed beyond words to be your mama.

To Great-Grandma Olive Wallace—

When others turned away, you immediately called us and prayed over us with a weeping fervor, speaking hope and God's wisdom into our darkest moments. You loved me as your own, and your eyes shone with His glory every time we spoke. Loving. Wise. Kind. Hopeful. At 106, you went home to the Lord, but the fruit in our lives today is rooted in your faithful prayers and steadfast intercession. Thank you for praying and leaving a godly legacy for generations to come.

To Delroy and Carol Wallace—

From the very first day of the shocking news, you stood beside us. You honored your son's courageous and noble choice to stay, meeting the moment with forgiveness, love, and hope—even when the road was hard. You were a steady source of encouragement for Craig through the toughest years. You were tender, loving grandparents to our children. Dad, you helped provide when finances were tight. Mummy, your kindness and gentleness toward me have been a constant gift, and I treasure the blessing of having a mother-in-love like you.

To Mary Giraldo—

Long before our paths crossed, your words found me in a prison cell—your letters carrying hope, stitched together by God's hand. He wove our stories into a tapestry of friendship, strong and loyal like David and Jonathan. You helped care for Tyson with love as I stepped into freedom, and now, fifteen years later, we still walk side by side—living, serving, and fighting the good fight together. We have shared joy and laughter, celebrated milestones, wept in the valleys, and stood shoulder to shoulder in prayer for our families. You are a rare and radiant jewel in my life, and I treasure the gift of your friendship as one of God's sweetest blessings!

To Gail Joy Hogue—

From the earliest days, when you changed my diapers, to the countless milestones we've celebrated, you have been a constant in my life. You have stood with me in seasons of victory and walked beside me through valleys of shadow. When my children were born, you drove seven hours from Pensacola, cradled them in your arms, and cared for them so Craig and I could rest. You came to see me in prison. When I was away, you poured love into Tyson—teaching him to swim, cheering him on, and giving him the steady presence of family. Selfless, loyal, and full of love, you are a rare and precious gift. More than a cousin, you have been like a sister to me all my life, and I thank God for the blessing of you.

To Melinda Garman and Lisa Patton— My very first women's bible study leaders, whose warmth and love carried me through the earliest, most uncertain days of my walk with Christ. You poured God's Word into my life, visited me in prison, and stood beside me when friends disappeared. Melinda, you prophetically confirmed the call to write this book in 2008, echoing the revelation God gave me in prison. You both laid foundations in my identity in Christ and modeled a church that loves instead of shames. The seeds you sowed in my life will bear fruit for His Kingdom for generations.

To Craig and Debbie Altman—

Twenty years ago, my husband and I sat in the second row when Grace Family Church was the size of today's children's ministry room. Today—eight campuses and a worldwide online family later—we've grown up here, served here, raised our children here, and found our true spiritual home.

Pastor Craig, your humility, authenticity, and steady boldness drew us in, but it was the way God spoke through you—clear, simple, and rich with His Word—that changed our lives. Our testimony is proof of the grace and love that flows through the people of this church.

It's no coincidence you and my husband share the same name, or that we share the same anniversary date—God writes the best stories. And Debbie, your heart for women and the godly wisdom you share have been such an inspiration. May generations be blessed because of your sacrificial commitment to start Grace Family Church to reach the lost, make disciples, and make Jesus known.

To Joe Diange—

Joe, you are the very picture of a faithful servant. When Craig and I first gave our lives to Christ, you were leading the New Believer's class at Grace Family Church. That first night, about twenty people attended. But as the weeks went on, it ended up being just the two of us—week after week. In church life, it's easy to measure success by numbers, but God knew exactly what we needed in that season. You gave us your undivided attention at a time when we were baby Christians in the middle of a fierce storm. You showed up without fail, pouring His word into us and laying some of the strongest foundations of truth in our faith.

We had so many questions, and you patiently loved us, led us, prayed for us, and continually pointed us back to the Word of God for answers. Though we haven't seen you in years, I pray God's hand of blessing and favor rests on you for the time you said "yes" to His call—*even if it was just for two people.*

To RV and Frances Brown—

RV, it was a divine appointment the day you were a guest speaker at Grace Family Church. Your bold proclamation of the gospel gripped our hearts and minds, pulling us from the very pits of hell—and we have never been the same since. I'll never forget how you looked into my eyes, tears of joy in yours, and you spoke the affirmation of a Heavenly Father I had never received from my earthly one. In that moment, it felt as though heaven itself split open, and God's love, grace, and forgiveness consumed my heart.

Frances, you are a pillar in the church—faithful as a wife, mother, and grandmother, a source of wise counsel, an encourager, and the giver of the very best hugs. Thank you both for your tireless dedication to the lost, to prisoners, to the youth, and for standing boldly and unashamed for the gospel. Your lives have left an eternal mark on ours. Two of your crowns in heaven will be from leading Craig and me to Christ! Glory, Glory, Glory!

To Doug and Marilyn Hinders—

You were our very first touchpoint at Grace Family Church, and from the moment we met, your love for Jesus shone through every action and every word. You hardly knew us, yet your unshakable faith in the God you serve led you to *know* He would redeem our story.

For years, you counseled us—with empathy, compassion, and at times, hard truth spoken in love. You prayed heaven open more times than we can count, standing firmly on God's promises for our lives. You spoke words that shattered fear and gave us courage. You supported us even when persecution came from both inside the church and outside in the world. You stood up for us in court when the media tried to destroy us.

Doug, you faithfully sent weekly emails filled with God's Word and hope. Marilyn, you wrote to me nonstop for two and a half years while I was in prison. So often, the exact verse or paragraph you sent arrived at just the right time. You always called me your "Paulina," as we wrote "epistles" back and forth, and your words pulled me out of fear and despair more times than I can count.

Your love didn't stop when I came home. Life after prison was hard, but you remained steadfast. Now in your seventies (or maybe even eighties!), you have been spiritual parents to both Craig and me, a gift we will cherish forever. Marilyn, you connected me to some of my dearest friends to serve in prison ministry together, and to women like Melinda Garman and Patricia Barr—each of whom God has used to shape me into the woman I am today. Doug, thank you for every meeting with Craig, for encouraging and loving him during our most difficult marriage seasons.

We could not have made it without your radical obedience to love us so well. I pray you are blessed beyond measure all the days of your lives.

To Dean and Kelli Wilde—

Shortly after we got saved, you shepherded us—our pastors and leaders in that very first married couples group at Grace Family Church. You loved us with a steady, Christlike love that supported our young steps in faith. Dean you came to the hospital shortly after Tyson was born, and you were among the first to hold and pray over him. Kelli, you were the first to sit with me in my brokenness from the abortion, guiding me with a gentleness that disarmed shame, an empathy that spoke of God's heart, and a kindness that wrapped around my soul.

For over two decades, you have encouraged our family— not just with words, but with the living testimony of your own lives, clinging to Jesus through the fiercest fires. Today, we honor you. We thank God for the counsel, the friendship, and the unwavering love you've poured into our story.

To Mike and Glenda Moore—

Just five years ago, we joined you in helping open the Land O' Lakes Grace Family Church campus. Mike, you've been like the protective big brother—or father— unafraid to stand firm in the face of criticism for allowing me to lead in the church despite my past. You have championed the heart of the gospel, standing on the truth that *the new is here, the old is gone*, and that a person is known by their fruit, not their history. You have affirmed, edified, and fearlessly had more difficult conversations on my behalf than most. You honored my sister's life after she passed, and you've consistently loved our family well.

Glenda, you serve with a radiant smile every time I see you, always intentional to connect and check in on my life. You may often work behind the scenes, but Jesus is always seen through you. Together, you live out an inspiring commitment to *be* the church in every part of your lives.

To Kristin Bonham—

You brought the *Freedom* study to our church, and I was in that very first group. It was there that God reached deep into my soul—breaking chains, breathing hope, and igniting a fire to see others set free. My identity in Christ became solid. The freedom I tasted was life-altering!

This was a starting point where my testimony was sharpened, my gifts stirred, and my calling fanned into my identity. You paid the price in prayer and warfare so that hundreds could encounter the same breakthrough. Because of your pioneer leadership, I stepped into guiding others through their freedom journey, and I've watched lives transformed before my eyes.

Not long ago, we sat in a coffee shop. I was weary, deep in the trenches of spiritual battles. You prayed over me, over this very book, and your words breathed courage into my spirit. Thank you for being a voice of the Lord in my life and a protector of His people. I am so grateful for you, your leadership, and your obedience!

To Patricia Barr—

You were a shepherd to my young mama heart as one of my first Bible study leaders who helped shape me into a woman after God's own heart, a faithful wife, and a loving mother. You spoke wisdom into our lives like streams of living water, and you prayed over our wombs as sacred vessels of His promise. You rejoiced with me in seasons of life, hosting my baby shower, and you wept with me in seasons of loss, ensuring meals and comfort when my arms felt empty.

Your home became a sanctuary—walls filled with prayer, laughter, fellowship, and the fragrance of the Word. In those formative years, you showed me not just how to study Proverbs 31, but how to *live* it, with grace that could only come from Him. For those sacred, shaping years, I thank God for you.

To Dwane and Indera Cardenas—

We met in that very first married couples small group, and from that day on, you've been some of our dearest friends. We raised our kids side by side, and you stepped in for Craig to help care for Tyson when I was in prison—always ready, always willing. You've become family to us in the truest sense, so much so that if we were ever called home to heaven "early," we would trust you to continue raising our children in the ways of the Lord.

From serving together at church to sharing Bible studies, BBQs, holidays, game nights, pool parties, family celebrations, and countless prayers, our families have been intertwined in both joy and trial. You've been there for us every time we reached out—through laughter and tears, through mountaintops and desperate valleys. Thank you for being some of the realest friends we could ever hope for, steady in love and unwavering in faith. Together, we've witnessed God move in miraculous ways in both our families, and we treasure your family as an inseparable part of our own story.

To Rolanda Beacham, Leilani Southern, Antonia Batista, Mary Giraldo, Tanisha Taylor—

We first connected as the core leadership team for prison ministry, but God quickly wove our lives into something far more: an unshakable sisterhood. Fresh out of prison, you saw His hand on my life and became my fiercest cheerleaders, faithful prayer warriors, and beloved sisters in Christ. You never once judged my past. Instead, you embraced God's testimony of grace in my story with fervent joy. We've laughed about being "Half Hood and Half Holy," because we all know the depths from which He rescued all of us—and that we stand where we are only by His mercy.

For nearly two decades, you've shown me authenticity, humility, and courage, inspiring me as you boldly follow Jesus through whatever life brings. I treasure our yearly birthday beach getaways—sharing our struggles, celebrating His goodness—and I hope we're still doing it in our 80s! I thank God for your friendship now and always!

To Jan McKee—

I still remember that first *Freedom Encounter*—hundreds of people in the sanctuary, and yet God had me wait in your prayer line. I didn't know it then, but He was weaving something far deeper than a single moment of prayer. Fifteen years later, you would not only become one of the content editors of this book, but a steady voice of godly counsel, pouring wisdom into my calling so others could meet Jesus and taste His chain-breaking freedom.

You've walked with me through the heat of spiritual battle, reminding me who I am and whose I am when the fight felt fierce. Though you carry titles, degrees, and credentials that could set you apart, you've chosen the way of humility—loving, listening, and carrying the burdens of those you counsel with compassion. Every conversation with you has been a divine appointment—God speaking through you to drop a word of knowledge, confirm a direction, or uncover the enemy's schemes. You are more than a friend, more than an editor. You are a gift to me and to the body of Christ!

To Ginnie Zemaitis—

We met in the most ordinary of places—the church bathroom on a random Tuesday morning after Bible study—yet it was anything but ordinary. A divine appointment in disguise. We started talking about Jesus and couldn't stop. You spoke of your passion for discipling youth, and something in my spirit knew this conversation was the beginning of more than friendship.

Over coffee, vision began to take shape. Through your leadership, my husband and I started a 7x7 youth Bible study in our home to help Tyson and his friends grow in Christ. You joined the *Freedom* class I was leading, and one day you suggested I join your 7x7 leadership team to help with leadership development and curriculum.

I was hesitant—fearful, even—to share my testimony, certain my past would disqualify me. But when you read it, you didn't flinch. You looked at me with joy and said, "I love that you went to prison! You're like Paul!" Then you poured out a prophetic word—six minutes long—that called out my identity, my assignment, and Jesus' heart for me. In that moment, you became more than a friend. You became a prayer partner, encourager, and a sister for life.

We've prayed through tears and groans for our families, stood on God's promises when the enemy came roaring, and watched Him move in ways that only He could. Ginnie, your love, grace, faith, and obedience have been a driving force in this season. Though you've only been in my life for four short years, it feels like a lifetime of blessings. You carry a greater passion for salvation and discipleship than anyone I know, and it inspires me daily. Thank you for everything you've poured into my life. Until God calls us home, may every breath of our vapor be all about Him.

To Phyllis Tarbox—

Ten years ago, you were the keynote speaker at a women's retreat where I was also presenting. I remember sitting in the front row, completely captivated by every word you spoke, because I knew without a doubt that the Holy Spirit was speaking directly to me. In that moment, it was as if Jesus Himself leaned in and confirmed, *"Jaymee, this is for you. This is your assignment. You will be set free, and then I will call you to be a vessel of the Holy Spirit to bring freedom to others through the authority and power of Jesus Christ."*

That encounter marked the beginning of a season of profound transformation in my life—healing, breakthrough, and the fruit of the Spirit became evident in ways that only God's grace could bring about. Your ministry was the spark that ignited so much of the victory I walk in today. I have sent countless men and women to your ministry, and their testimonies of freedom and renewal continue to bear lasting fruit.

Recently, I have been deeply grateful for the way you have counseled my husband and son through a difficult season. Thank you for your unwavering commitment to bring hope and freedom to the body of Christ. Your faithfulness has left an eternal mark not only on my life, but on the lives of many!

To Ricky Sr. and Beth Solomon—

Thank you so much for sending us sermon tapes, covering us in prayer, and encouraging us in countless ways when we first came to faith. Your love and faithfulness toward my husband, especially in the seasons when I was away, were truly the voice of the Holy Spirit speaking through you. Though you lived in another state, the way you stayed so intentionally connected really touched our hearts. Your care carried us through some of the hardest times—both before and after I went to prison—and for that we will always be deeply grateful.

Cristina Vega Johnston—

Our paths first crossed six years ago when you stepped into leadership within our women's ministry at church, and from the very beginning you brought such a bright light of sunshine to our community! Not long after, God called you beyond the church walls to carry out His divine assignments, and yet, in His perfect timing, He reconnected us this past year. What a gift it has been to walk with you again as both a sister in Christ and a dear friend.

Our fellowship and prayer time has felt like heaven itself opening over us, and I treasure your zeal and unshakable excitement for kingdom work. You're that friend who says, "Let me bless you—whether it's a massage, a meal, or a coffee," because you're so in tune with the weight of the assignment and wanted to lighten the load.

And now, here we are once again, our paths divinely intersecting through your powerful Christian networking ministry for women and the launch of this book. Thank you for your obedience, your steadfast friendship, and the countless ways you've blessed me. I pray God's anointing and favor continue to rest upon you as you fulfill every calling He has placed on your life. Glory, glory, glory!

To Carina DesHotels—

Not only have we had fifteen beautiful years of friendship since first meeting at MOPS, but God has also intricately woven our ministry paths together for such a time as this. Thank you for serving as one of my content editors on the original manuscript of this book—your encouragement, thoughtful feedback, and honest reflections helped shape my words into something that could truly connect with the reader. I deeply admire your humility, your love for people, and your unwavering desire to seek and obey Him in all things. What a gift it is to call you friend and to walk side by side in the divine assignments God has entrusted to us. You are a blessing beyond measure!

To Diane Engelhardt and Elaine Woods—

Though our time of knowing one another has been short, I have no doubt God placed you on my path for this very assignment—to fan the flames of encouragement I so desperately needed. You embody the heart of Titus women, faithfully loving and imparting wisdom to younger women as they step into their callings. Your sincere words, your warm hugs, and even the tears that accompanied your affirmations gave me courage to persevere. Thank you for lending your heart and insight as content editors of the first manuscript, and for continuing to pray with all your strength that Jesus would be lifted high through this testimony. May the blessings you've poured out return to your family for generations to come!

To Ivory Granger—

It was no accident that our paths collided as we worshiped side by side among 1,500 women. When I walked into a *Freedom* group to share, there you were again! From that divine intersection, God knit together a beautiful friendship—a true sister in Christ to intercede with, to spur one another on in our giftings and purpose, and to walk together in the calling of a modern-day Deborah.

I am deeply grateful for your passion for soul care, your boldness to use your prophetic gifts to awaken God's people, and the way your voice shines like warm sunshine—even when speaking truth in love. Thank you for warring with me week after week through these last two years of writing this book. You've been in the trenches with me—full of empathy, compassion, and encouragement—praying through every ugly and hard moment, breathing fresh air into my weary soul when I wanted to quit.

I love you like a sister, and I know this is only the beginning of our aligned assignments, testimonies, and giftings for His glory. I pray an Ephesians 3:20 blessing over your marriage, your children, and every way God chooses to use you—exceedingly, abundantly, beyond all you could ask or imagine!

To Shannon Guzman, Misty Umholtz, Allison Marks, Denise Horne, Joshua Giles—

Prophets: a word fitly spoken. Each of you walks in such a powerful anointing to be His messengers with holy boldness. God entrusted you with dreams, visions, prophetic words, and prayers that you faithfully shared with me about my assignment—each one like manna from heaven, delivered in the perfect moment. Thank you for your obedience to speak and to pray, confirming what God Himself was bringing to pass in my life.

The beauty of your giftings is the way you steward them—with humility, purity, and a burning desire to glorify Jesus above all else. There is no striving, only full submission to the will of the Father. Through you, I have received revelations that go far beyond this book, igniting a fire in my spirit to walk boldly down every path He sets before me. He continues to confirm the words spoken through His word.

May you continue to be prophetic voices in this generation, aligning the church with His perfect will. May His holy fire consume the works of the enemy through your intercession, and may you walk fully in all He has ordained for you. I am profoundly grateful for your commitment to the Kingdom of God. Keep sounding the trumpet without fear of man! Glory to God!

To our Tuesday morning intercessory prayer team: Ashley McNally, Dana Spears, Laura Ernst, Lindsey Powell, Cherise Katsaros, Trudy Loots, Ginnie Zemaitis, Ivory Granger, Shannon Guzman, Denise Horne—

What a priceless gift it has been to gather with you week after week—interceding for the church, our children, our marriages, our assignments, our purity of heart, our healing, and for the lost. Together we stood in agreement for God's perfect will to be fulfilled on earth. Each Tuesday morning your prayers touched heaven and transformed our hearts as we fervently followed the leading of the Spirit.

Thank you for being true repairers of the breach—standing in the gap, testifying of God's faithfulness, and calling forth His promises. And how could we ever forget our first outing, when Carrabba's was transformed into a house of prayer and healing!

Your leadership, service, and unwavering dedication to commune with the Almighty has been a treasure beyond words. I believe much of this book was written as a result of your prayers. It has been an honor to pray alongside you.

To all the 7x7 (Apologetics Discipleship Home Bible Study) parents and students who allowed me and my husband to lead and disciple the past five years—

You embraced me and Craig like family, partnering with us in the sacred work of discipling your young adults. Thank you for the prayers, the meals, the hospitality, and most of all, the grace you extended in allowing me to lead your teens despite my past. Where others might have disqualified me, you stood firmly on the power of testimony and the eternal seeds it would sow in the hearts of young disciples.

To the students, after five years of journeying together, we finally shared our testimony. Though it may have been shocking, your response was nothing short of remarkable. You expressed how it emboldened you to share your own stories without shame, and how it deepened your faith in the transforming power of the gospel. We are both humbled and honored to have been part of your faith journey. And now, we eagerly wait with expectant hearts to see God's Spirit and a harvest explode through your lives in college and far beyond!

To Indwanai Cardenas—

To our beloved god-daughter, known and loved by us since before you were born. We first met your parents in Bible study, and here we are, twenty years later, our families woven together as true family.

Thank you for being such a faithful friend to our son, Tyson, especially during the seasons of deep persecution he faced because of my testimony. You have been an unwavering friend. You listened, you loved, and you stood with him as he wrestled through hard conversations and the weight of warfare coming against us.

You have been a compassionate light to him, and to us, and for that I am endlessly grateful—for your prayers, your steadfast heart, and your desire to see Jesus at work in it all. You are a rare and radiant gem! I know there is more kingdom work for our families to do together, and I cannot wait to watch God unfold the chapters still to come. May your life continue to shine brightly for His glory, and may every step you take be marked by His favor and faithfulness.

To Heather Thompson—

My ultimate hype girl! You embody Jersey and Jesus in every way, and that's exactly why I treasure our friendship. You make us all laugh while bringing a fiery passion for making Jesus known everywhere you go. Who would have thought that when you first walked into my hip-hop class, God was already orchestrating a divine sisterhood? The enemy tried to use my past to push you away, but God had already prepared your heart for His gospel.

I'll never forget when you surrendered your life to Christ at our women's conference, and then dove headfirst into my Wednesday night Bible study. What a joy it has been to watch your transformation unfold before my very eyes! Your testimony is powerful, and I believe the world needs to hear it. If anyone is going to carry stacks of this book into the streets, it will be you—evangelizing like the woman at the well, boldly declaring the goodness of our God.

Thank you for your constant support, your love, and your contagious excitement to share what Jesus has done in our lives. Your childlike faith and zeal for the Lord inspire me more than words can say. I am beyond grateful to have you in my corner. I can't wait to see the day when that "Jersey and Jesus" podcast comes to life! I pray His goodness and mercy follow you all the days of your life!

To Wednesday Night Bible Study ladies - Christine Moore, Sarah Weidman, Heather Thompson, Aly Zapata, Cori Cassilly, Madison Johnson, Liona Brown, Dezzie Sala—

Our shared love for dance, fitness, and motherhood first brought our paths together, but it was God's greater story to grow in Christ together. Each of you said *yes* to joining Bible study because of the testimony in this book, and my prayer is that you will boldly share the goodness of God through your own stories to everyone you encounter.

I have watched the Lord draw you to His well of living water, seeking Jesus and asking your questions of faith. What a joy it has been to watch the Holy Spirit meet you right where you are and reveal His love and plan for your life! Thank you for your prayers and encouragement over the years as I labored to write and finish this book. It truly became the "never-ending prayer request." In my living room, we have shared so many tears, prayers, laughter, and moments of fellowship. What a gift you are to me—fun, inspiring, and faithful sisters in Christ. I am forever grateful for your friendship, and I pray that you will continue to follow Jesus with all your hearts for every day of your lives!

To Susie Walther—

You are such a powerhouse in women's ministry, and I am deeply grateful for your leadership in my life and your passion for authentic discipleship in the Body of Christ. Your *Renovated Wives Conference* wrecked me—in the best way—and your prayers over me, this book, and God's divine assignments have refreshed my soul and breathed hope into seasons of discouragement. Thank you for your courage, your resilience, and your relentless pursuit of fanning the flame in countless women of God. You are a living example of staying faithful to the mission He has entrusted to you, never shrinking back in fear of man. Truly, you are a force to be reckoned with for the Kingdom of God. I pray His portion is multiplied over your calling a hundredfold!

To Stephan & Feli Joseph—

You will always hold a special place in my heart because you were the first to invite me to share my testimony with an audience of strangers in your church. Thank you for your unashamed boldness in giving space for the hope and gospel of Jesus Christ—the very gospel that transformed my life—to be proclaimed to those you were shepherding.

That moment was life-changing for me. I watched as the Holy Spirit moved mightily, grabbing hold of hurting and broken hearts, flooding the room with light that extinguished the darkness. Where fear of judgment could have silenced my story and the weight of my sin might have screamed "unworthy," you did not bow to fear—not for a moment. I pray a special blessing over your family and your ministry. May you continue to use your influence to release redemption stories, to lead many to Jesus, and to usher countless souls into victory. Glory, glory, glory!

To Luisa Mayer & the Tuesday Morning Beautiful Leadership Team—

Luisa, we first crossed paths in a homeschool group 15 years ago, and then—by God's perfect timing—our seasons reunited six years ago as we helped open another church campus together. What a gift it has been to walk alongside you in women's ministry all these years. Thank you for your steadfast leadership, your listening ear, and the spiritual maturity you've poured into so many of us. Your encouragement has been a lifeline to countless women you've led and loved so well.

To the Land O' Lakes Tuesday morning leadership team—you have each been such a blessing in my journey. Thank you for your prayers, your willingness to say "yes" to stewarding the women God has entrusted to you, and for cultivating a community of leaders who truly sharpen one another. I pray you continue to boldly walk out every assignment the Lord has placed before you, and that together, you will raise up a generation of new disciples on fire for Jesus!

To the "Angels" in Blue that I did my time with: Jennifer C, Mindy B., MJ, Jackie H., Glenda H., Staci M, Melinda C., Maureen M., Sonya C, Rosa B., SaRina M. —

No one can truly understand the prison world unless they've walked through it themselves. Thank you for the love, support, and laughter that helped me endure that season. Whether it was dance classes at rec, worshipping and praying in the chapel, or simply spending time together in the dorm, you made my life brighter and more bearable there. No matter how much time passes or how far apart we may be, we will always share a bond of survival and overcoming— my sisters, the angels in blue. My prayer is that wherever you are today, you know this truth: you are chosen, forgiven, loved, and accepted. God longs to redeem and restore all that has been lost, and He desires to use your story for His glory, too. All He's waiting for is your heart—whether to return to Him or to seek Him for the very first time. I am deeply grateful for each of you.

To Laura Lonero—

Our boys first met in VPK fourteen years ago, and little did we know how God would so beautifully intertwine our lives— through friendship, raising kids side by side, and even through the countless times the Holy Spirit spoke powerfully to one another while you cut and colored my hair!

Thank you for every prayer session and for blessing me— and so many others—with your angelic voice that ushers in the very presence of God wherever you sing. I pray you lay every gift He has anointed you with at His feet, so He can astonish you with the arenas of souls who will come to know Jesus and be set free through your prophetic songs. Your testimony carries weight and power, and when God completes His refining fire, you will emerge as pure gold for His glory. Thank you for your encouragement and for speaking God's promises over me and this book. You truly are a gift!

To Apologetics Inc. Staff & Board—

Thank you for your faithful prayers every Wednesday, covering both me and the completion of this book. Your kind and encouraging words have blessed me, and you all are a witness to God's goodness and faithfulness—even when His assignments take us on unexpected detours that don't align with "our plans." His are always better.

Each of you inspires me with your unwavering commitment to proclaim that Christ and Christianity are true and good. I am especially grateful for the ways you have challenged me to love Jesus with all of my mind and for expanding my knowledge of the tsunami of evidence that affirms Jesus is exactly who He says He is. I pray God continues to open your eyes to the wonder of His presence & power, and that He uses each of you mightily for His glory!

To Harley Riedel, Kara Kennedy, and Dave Engelhardt—

When God shifted my assignment to writing this book, I could have never imagined how He would also provide the resources to see it through. Your "yes" to sowing seed into this kingdom work has humbled me deeply. I am honored to witness the harvest that will flow from your faithful generosity. Words like "thank you" hardly capture the depth of my gratitude. I pray that the hand of God will pour out blessings upon your businesses, ministries, and families—beyond measure—so His work may continue on earth as it is in heaven. You truly have been a blessing beyond words!

To Ben and Havilah Cunnington—

It was such a God-orchestrated moment when I received Havilah's text inviting me to author school the very same week I realized I needed structure and accountability to write this book. Over 16 weeks, you and your team poured into me with wisdom, prayer, encouragement, and a wealth of knowledge and resources that equipped me as a first-time author. Your guidance gave me the confidence and clarity to finish my first manuscript. You are truly top-notch in your field, and it's evident that God is at the center of all you do. I pray you continue to raise up a generation of authors who will proclaim the gospel, make Jesus known, and boldly share the messages He has written on the tablets of their hearts!

To My Author Mastermind Group: Celena Higgins, Alyssa Wandrey, Sara O'Connell, & Erin—

Out of a hundred people in the author school, God knit our paths together to write our first books. From the far corners of the earth—Canada, Florida, California, and Australia—He united us to share stories of His healing, redemption, and unfailing love. Each of our testimonies is unique, yet woven together by the same unshakable truth: **Jesus changes everything.** Week after week, we laughed, cried, prayed, and bared our most vulnerable chapters so His message of hope could shine through.

Thank you for your feedback, wisdom, encouragement, and the courage to share what God has done in your life. I pray that, whatever stage you are in on this publishing journey, you will finish the assignment God has entrusted to you. From your mother's womb, you were called as messengers to the nations, testifying of His goodness. Truly, Deborahs with pens!

To Dave Engelhardt—

We first met in late 2020, during an interview to bring me on staff to work alongside Ginnie in writing curriculum and training new leaders in ministry. From that moment on, you have been such a blessing—encouraging, praying, leading, and offering wisdom at every turn over these last years.

Ginnie and I lovingly call you our "Spiritual Dad Dave," and it's no small detail that both of our earthly fathers were also named David. Though we didn't receive the spiritual covering we longed for from our earthly dads, God provided it through your obedience and love for Jesus.

The road to this point has had its share of bumps, but you never once stopped fighting for God's assignment in my life. You remained steadfast, fully confident that God would rewrite my story to be used for the expansion of His Kingdom, Jesus would be glorified, and healing would come to so many lost and broken. Thank you, Dave, for your prayers, your faith, your generosity, and your unwavering heart for God's purposes through my life. May you and Diane be abundantly blessed in every way. Love you both dearly.

To Kara Kennedy—

Oh, my sweet sister in Christ, what a divine appointment it was when God first connected us as you served on the board of the ministry I worked for. Once again, His sovereign hand was aligning our stories together for greater purposes. You and your husband, Juan, graciously opened your home to host our 7x7 Discipleship group, teaching our youth the richness of Jewish culture and how it beautifully deepens our walk as Christians.

You were part of that sacred moment in the boardroom when the Holy Spirit shifted my assignment, confirming the very word God had spoken to me years ago in that prison chapel—to write this book. Since that day, you have poured out prayers, resources, encouragement, and wisdom, standing faithfully with me—zealous, loving, and unwavering in your belief in what the Lord would do.

Kara, you are so much more than your incredible accomplishments—author, speaker, entrepreneur, Harvard graduate, and countless other accolades. What shines most brightly is your humility, your kindness, and your deep love for Jesus. I am beyond blessed to have you as an integral part of this journey. My gratitude for you stretches as wide as the sky.

Thank you for everything—for your friendship, your faithfulness, and for the beautiful foreword you wrote to help usher the reader to receive from the Lord. I pray God's abundant provision, grace, love, and hope over your life, your family, and every endeavor you put your hands to—all for His glory!

To my editor, Melody Farrell—

I am in awe of our God! I know without a doubt He handpicked you to come alongside me in these final finishing touches for His glory. Through Kara's connections in the literary and publishing world, what a gift from heaven it was that God brought you into this project! Though we've only met through Zoom, I have been amazed at how God has used both your expertise and the guidance of His Spirit to shape this book. More than once, I've sat back, looked at the finished pages, and whispered, "Wow, Lord... look what You did!"

Over these last six months, we have worked like two peas in a pod—submitting together to God's will for what He wanted to say and do through this memoir. Your dedication, commitment, and wisdom allowed Jesus to shine through every page. You brought a seamless flow to the story while sharpening the edges to leave an even greater impact on the reader. I am grateful for your attention to detail and for honoring my voice.

You are also the very first person to read this book without knowing me personally, or the "Jaymee" I am today. Yet your response to the testimony—so full of hope, love, conviction, grace, and encouragement—spoke volumes about your own deep love for Jesus.

Melody, you have been such a blessing. It has been an honor and a joy to work with you. I pray that you will continue to use your gifts in every project and in every season! Thank you so much!

DISCUSSION GUIDE ACCESS

Link to **www.thehealinghubministry.com** for access to chapter-by-chapter discussion questions for use in Bible Study and Small Groups, available now!

The *Selah Moments* resource will be available soon!

Jaymee Lane Wallace lives in Tampa Bay, Florida, with her husband of twenty-two years, Craig, and their two children, Tyson Isaiah and Trinity Marie. Jaymee and Craig lead an in-home discipleship group for young adults, teaching God's Word, answering tough faith questions, and encouraging them to walk the narrow road with Christ despite cultural pressures. Passionate about equipping others to live in freedom, Jaymee has served as a Bible study leader, curriculum writer, and women's ministry leader. She also enjoys teaching hip-hop and weightlifting classes, cheering on her kids at soccer, coffee with friends, and outdoor adventures with her husband.

To book Jaymee as a speaker and access all bonus resources, visit
www.thehealinghubministry.com

Follow Jaymee on
Instagram: @Jaymee_Lane
Facebook: Jaymee Lane